THUS SAYS THE LORD

THE PROPHETS IN THE LITURGY

LITURGY
AND THE
BIBLE

RICHARD J. CLIFFORD, SJ

LTP

LITURGY
TRAINING
PUBLICATIONS

Nihil Obstat
Rev. Mr. Daniel G. Welter, JCL
Chancellor
Archdiocese of Chicago
May 11, 2021

Imprimatur
Most Rev. Robert G. Casey
Vicar General
Archdiocese of Chicago
May 11, 2021

The *Nihil Obstat* and *Imprimatur* are declarations that the material is free from doctrinal or moral error, and thus is granted permission to publish in accordance with c. 827. No legal responsibility is assumed by the grant of this permission. No implication is contained herein that those who have granted the *Nihil Obstat* and *Imprimatur* agree with the content, opinions, or statements expressed.

Cover: see p. 122; p. 13: Wellcome Collection / Wikimedia Commons; p. 54: Cancre / Wikimedia Commons; p. 73: Richard Mortel / Wikimedia Commons; p. 101: Levan Ramishvili / Wikimedia Commons.

THUS SAYS THE LORD: THE PROPHETS IN THE LITURGY © 2021 Archdiocese of Chicago: Liturgy Training Publications, 3949 South Racine Avenue, Chicago, IL 60609; 800-933-1800; fax: 800-933-7094; email: orders@ltp.org; website: www.LTP.org. All rights reserved.

This book is part of the *Liturgy and the Bible* series.

This book was edited by Lorie Simmons. Christian Rocha was the production editor, Anna Manhart was the designer, and Juan Alberto Castillo was the production artist.

25 24 23 22 21   1 2 3 4 5

Printed in the United States of America

Library of Congress Control Number: 2021938567

ISBN: 978-1-61671-640-0

LBPL

To my colleagues and my students at
Weston Jesuit School of Theology (1970–2007)
and in Weston Jesuit's new identity as the
Boston College School of Theology and Ministry
(2008–forward).

"On that day . . . the Lord of Hosts will bless them, saying,
'Blessed be My people Egypt, My handiwork Assyria, and
My very own Israel.'"

Isaiah 19:25 (New Jewish Publication Society translation)

❖

CONTENTS

ABBREVIATIONS

1QIsaᵃ   A standard abbreviation for the Dead Sea Scrolls. First of the Isaiah scrolls found in Cave 1 at Qumran.

ANET   *Ancient Near Eastern Texts Relating to the Old Testament,* ed. J. B. Pritchard, 3rd ed. (Princeton, NJ: Princeton University Press, 1969).

LXX   The Septuagint, a Greek translation of the Hebrew text made by Jews in the third and second centuries BC.

MT   Masoretic Text, the Hebrew text curated by the Masoretes, Jewish scholars of the sixth to the tenth centuries AD. The Ben Asher family gave the textual tradition its final form.

NABRE   New American Bible Revised Edition (2011).

NJPS   New Jewish Publication Society translation (1970).

NRSV   New Revised Standard Version (1970).

Getting to Know the Prophets and Notes about Translations

The Often-Misunderstood Prophets

This book aims to help people understand the Hebrew prophets who frequently speak in the liturgy through the Catholic lectionary. It can serve Protestant Christians as well, for the Revised Common Lectionary used in many Protestant churches (which incorporated the Common Lectionary of 1983 and the Consultation on Church Union Lectionary of 1974) originally drew on the 1969 three-year Catholic lectionary launched after the Second Vatican Council.

Catholics, many of whom do not read the Bible regularly, usually derive their understanding of the Bible from hearing the readings at Mass. Though it's possible to pick up a few commonplaces about the Hebrew prophets from the lectionary—for example, the prophets' care for the widow and the orphan, and their concern for right worship—these don't provide the knowledge necessary to understand the prophets' deeper messages. They can even create false impressions—for example, that the prophets were always angry or were obsessed with details of worship irrelevant to modern life.

The reality, however, is entirely different. The prophets loved God deeply; they were convinced that God loved his people and was moved by their suffering. God was angered only by their rebellion. Above all, God wanted Israel to flourish and show the world what happens to a nation that is faithful to their Lord.

Prophetic texts in the lectionary show us the Lord's demands, to be sure, but they show even more the Lord's passionate commitment and faithfulness to Israel and astonishing acceptance of weak and inconsistent human beings. "Can a mother forget her infant, / . . . Even should she forget, / I will never forget you" (Isaiah 49:15, Eighth Sunday, year A). The prophets detach Christians from their comforting illusions, "Two evils have my people done: / they have forsaken me, the source of living waters; / They have dug themselves cisterns, / broken cisterns, that hold no water" (Jeremiah 2:13, Sixteenth Week, Thursday, year 2). If we heed the prophets in the lectionary, they will help us see God's dream for Israel and for the world, "For I am God and not man, / the Holy One present among you; / I will not let the flames consume you" (Hosea 11:9, Fourteenth Week, Thursday, year 2).

The prophets interpreted the reality around them, even when that reality was discomforting. When Isaiah of Jerusalem quoted the Lord sending the notoriously cruel Assyrian Empire to chastise Israel, "Ah, Assyria, the rod of my anger— / the club in their hands is my fury!" (Isaiah 10:5, NRSV),[1] the message frightened him, but it was not the whole story. The lectionary (Fifteenth Week, Wednesday, year 2) pairs it with a New Testament passage, Matthew 11:25–27 , which situates the Isaian verse in the context of God's inscrutable yet kindly governance, for Jesus says in Matthew, "I give praise to you, Father, Lord of heaven and earth, for although you have hidden these things from the wise and the learned, you have revealed them to the childlike" (verse 25). The pairing suggests that a vengeful God is not unleashing a brutal army in order to torture his own people, but rather is assuring Israel that even in terrifying situations, God can still be found and God's plan be followed.

At first glance, some prophetic texts in the lectionary seem unconnected to the accompanying New Testament passages. To be sure, lectionary pairings can puzzle even experienced readers. The main point of all the prophetic passages, however, is that the Word of

---

1. The lectionary version of this passage is: "Woe to Assyria! My rod in anger, / my staff in wrath."

God drives history forward; there is a design in God's plan, even if that design is not obvious to us.

Prophets in Biblical History

Prophets appear in the Bible in three clusters. The first is the prophets in the eleventh- and tenth-centuries, when there was a transition in the way Israel was ruled—from judges to kings. The second cluster includes two larger-than-life individuals—the ninth-century prophets Elijah and Elisha. The third cluster is the largest, most well-known group: the writing prophets, whose texts appear in the Bible. This third group of prophets engages with the dissolution (often called the exile) and eventual restoration of Israel that took place between 750 and 500 BC. Not every writing prophet prophesied during this period, nor was every prophet aware that those two-and-a-half centuries would eventually be seen as a whole. Zechariah 9–14 and Malachi, for example, seem to have come later, but the issues those prophets deal with arose in the earlier period. Jonah, of course, is fiction and impossible to date precisely, but even Jonah deals with the Assyrian Empire, Israel's eighth-century nemesis.

How This Book Will Present the Prophets

This book seeks to assist Christian congregations to hear and understand the prophets, both when they are proclaimed in the liturgy and when they are read privately. Chapter 1 reminds us that the Catholic lectionary, unchanged for centuries, has been radically revised and now includes a wide selection of biblical texts, especially texts from the Old Testament. Among the newly included texts are the Old Testament prophets, each accompanied by New Testament texts. New texts and old shed light on each other. Old Testament texts point forward, though they remain relevant to the situation that originally called them forth. New Testament texts develop themes already sounded in the Old Testament, bringing them to a conclusion or to a stage of further development.

Chapter 1 argues that texts from another time and culture must be interpreted if they are to make sense to us. Interpretation does not mean putting our "spin" on ancient texts. Rather, it invites us to reflect on how ancient texts provide meaning and consolation for today.

Chapter 2 covers recent trends in the study of the prophets and then gives a historical sketch of prophecy in Israel prior to the great writing prophets—the four Major Prophets and the twelve Minor Prophets—which will be our main interest.

Chapter 3 sketches all the Old Testament writing prophets except Isaiah (which deserves its own chapter). The chapter reviews the narratives and, above all, the preaching of the writing prophets, giving a sample of how the lectionary interprets them.

Chapter 4 deals exclusively with Isaiah. The book of Isaiah is the only prophetic book to interpret and monitor the entire process of judgment and restoration from 750 to 500 BC. Isaiah of Jerusalem in the eighth century recorded the beginning of the process; much of his preaching is contained in chapters 1–39. Almost two centuries later, about the middle of the sixth century, the judgment process of the nation came to its conclusion. An anonymous individual felt called to continue the ministry of Isaiah of Jerusalem and other prophets as well. He announced the conclusion of the judgment process and taught Israel how to respond to it. His words, and likely the words of other prophets, are contained in Isaiah 40–66. Because the book of Isaiah interprets the whole judgment process, and because the prophets who wrote it were such accomplished poets and theologians, it deserves a separate chapter.

Chapter 5 describes *how* the prophets wrote—that is, their rhetoric, forms, and genres. The conclusion views the history of Israel as three "exodus moments," each moment accompanied by prophetic voices that interpreted the moment and modeled a response.

Study Bibles—an Important Tool for Coming to Know the Prophets

A final word on reading the prophets. Since the publication in the 1950s of *La Bible de Jérusalem*, translated and annotated by the Dominican Fathers in France and the Holy Land, a flood of good annotated Bibles has appeared, enriching both Christians and Jews. I mention only a few of these Bibles: *The Catholic Study Bible, The Jewish Study Bible, The Oxford Annotated Bible, The HarperCollins Study Bible, The New Interpreter's Study Bible,* and *The CEB Study Bible.* All have the biblical text on the upper part of the page and brief notes at the bottom. The blend of text and modest comment has proven to be successful in helping readers focus on the biblical text with just enough comment to make the text understandable. Though hearing the prophets in the lectionary is an indispensable way for Christians to encounter them, hearers will be immeasurably enriched by reading the prophets privately, with scholars at the bottom of the page occasionally whispering in their ear.

What You Need to Know about Biblical Texts and English Translations

Hebrew Text

Masoretic Text (MT). The Hebrew text (including a few Aramaic passages), known to Christians as the Old Testament, is largely based on two medieval manuscripts: the Aleppo Codex (around AD 900) and the Leningrad Codex (around AD 1009). Because Hebrew is written in consonants only, it was accompanied by markings or notes about punctuation and pronunciation, which were displayed in these manuscripts. The notes, often referred to as "the consonantal textual tradition," were composed much earlier and fixed from the first century AD. Jewish scholars in Palestine and Babylonia, called Masoretes, were responsible for preserving that tradition from the seventh to the eleventh centuries. The Masoretic Text (MT) is so called from the term *Masorah*, which refers to the many instructions for writing and reading the biblical text written on the margins of that text.

Until the discovery of the Dead Sea Scrolls in 1947 at Qumran, the Aleppo and Leningrad codices were the oldest Hebrew witnesses to the Hebrew Bible. Versions in other languages were of course older: (1) the Greek Septuagint (abbreviated LXX and described below, from the third and second century BC), and translations done from the Septuagint such as (2) the translation known as the Old Latin (from the second century), which was largely replaced by (3) the Latin Vulgate (in the fourth century), and (4) the Peshitta or Syriac version (fifth century, perhaps earlier).

In 1947, the first of the Dead Sea Scrolls was discovered; they date from the mid-third century BC through AD 68. Of the approximately 930 documents found at Qumran, 230 are biblical manuscripts, representing every book of the Hebrew Bible except Esther, with Isaiah, Psalms, and Deuteronomy being the best represented (the same books quoted most often by the New Testament). The Scrolls are important because they attest to the extraordinary accuracy of the medieval Hebrew Bible manuscripts, and they enable us to chart the transmission of the Hebrew texts in their more fluid stage prior to the time they were fixed in the first century AD.

The Qumran scrolls are described by their names. For example, 1QIsaᵃ tells us that the scroll was found in Cave 1 (of the 11 caves at Qumran), that the document comes from Qumran (Q), that the manuscript is of the prophet Isaiah (Isa), and that it is distinct from other manuscripts of Isaiah(ᵃ).

The Septuagint (LXX). This Greek translation of the Hebrew text was done in the third and second centuries for Jews who did not know Hebrew. The term *Septuagint* is derived from a Greek word meaning "seventy," which referred to a traditional story that it was the work of seventy translators, in Roman numerals LXX. It is older than MT and sometimes offers superior readings. New Testament authors customarily quoted LXX rather than MT. Early Christian writers down to the later fourth century almost all regarded LXX as the standard form of the Old Testament, regarded it as inspired, and seldom referred to the Hebrew. It is still the canonical form of the Old Testament in the Eastern Orthodox Church.

Latin Vulgate (Vg). The Latin Bible has been in common use in the Western Church since the seventh century. It is not the work of one author, though most of the Old Testament books were translated by St. Jerome (345–420). In the New Testament, Jerome revised the earlier Old Latin Gospels, but other hands revised at least some of the Old Latin translations. Vg served as the standard Bible in the Western Church until modern times. The Council of Trent (1545–1563) declared the Latin Vulgate "authentic," which was later widely misunderstood as making the Vulgate the "official version of the Bible" for the Catholic Church. But as Pope Pius XII's encyclical *Divino afflante Spiritu* taught,[2] the designation "authentic" used at Trent meant only that among the myriad Bible translations of that era, Vg was a reliable text for preaching and teaching, to be revered because of its long usage in the Latin Church. The Council Fathers were well aware of the errors that had accrued to the Vulgate over the centuries. As at Trent, the writers of the Second Vatican Council's document *Dei Verbum* (*Dogmatic Constitution on Divine Revelation*)[3] acknowledged the venerable nature of the Vulgate but reaffirmed the teaching of the 1943 encyclical *Divino afflante Spiritu* that urged biblical scholars to translate the original Hebrew and Greek texts. Recent years have seen attempts to impose the Vulgate as a standard for translation, but they run counter to the directives of *Dei Verbum*.

Major English Translations

NABRE. The New American Bible Revised Edition is the 2011 revision of NAB, the New American Bible of 1970. It was produced by the Catholic Biblical Association of America (with some Protestant scholars) from the original languages. It is the first translation by Catholics

---

2. The document was promulgated in 1943. Its Latin title means "Inspired by the Divine Spirit," the first words of the document.

3. This document was promulgated in 1965. Its Latin title means "The Word of God," the first words of the document.

of the entire Bible from original biblical languages into English; prior to this translation, Catholic scholars translated the Bible from the Latin Vulgate. Unless otherwise indicated by the abbreviations listed below, most Scripture quoted in this book is from the NABRE. If I am referring specifically to a passage from the *Lectionary for Mass*, the quotation will come from the lectionary, which is based on, but not always identical to the NABRE.

NRSV (1989). The most commonly used Bible in the United States is the New Revised Standard Version, first published in 1989, produced by American Protestant scholars. It was intended to replace the Revised Standard Version (RSV), first published in 1946. The NRSV uses inclusive language to refer to humans. Both the RSV and NRSV follow the tradition of the revered seventeenth-century King James Version (KJV, also called the Authorized Version).

RNJB. The Revised New Jerusalem Bible (2019) is a British Catholic translation that continues the great tradition of *La Bible de Jérusalem* of the 1950s. The notes were translated from the French version, but the biblical text was translated afresh from the original languages.

OTHER RELIABLE ENGLISH TRANSLATIONS

NIV. New International Version (1973 subsequently revised)

CEB. The Common English Bible (2011), which uses everyday English.

NJPS. The New Jewish Publication Society Version (1970), an excellent translation of the Hebrew Bible, translated by Jewish scholars.

All of the translations of Scripture mentioned above have an annotated or study version; that is, they are equipped with short introductions to each book and notes at the bottom of each page.

I do not recommend the following Bibles as they are too free or uncritical: *The Way, The Living Bible, The New King James Bible, The Good News Bible,* and *The Contemporary English Version.* Also I do not recommend the annotated versions of *The English Standard Version* (ESV), which is fundamentalist and uncritical.

Chapter 1

Meeting the Prophets in the Liturgy and the Challenge of Interpretation

Meeting the Prophets in the Readings of the Mass

Catholics who are not regular readers of the Bible usually meet the prophets in the readings at Sunday Mass and, less directly, in Christian art and in hymns. Prior to the Second Vatican Council (1962–65), Catholic Mass-goers almost never heard the prophets read aloud in the liturgy. The lectionary (the official book containing the Bible readings for liturgical celebrations over the course of the year) remained substantially unchanged from 1570 to 1969; it contained only 118 verses from the prophets. A revision in 1951 reduced the verses even further, to less than half of one percent of the Old Testament! The readings for Sunday Mass contained not a single passage from the Old Testament! As part of its extensive reform of the Catholic liturgy, the bishops at the Second Vatican Council mandated a new lectionary for Mass, which came out in English in 1970. But even the revision in its first edition contained only 3.7 percent of the Old Testament. The second edition of the Lectionary (1998, 2002) inserted new Masses and more Old Testament readings, raising the percentage to 13.5 percent. Though still small when one considers the massive size of the Old Testament, it is certainly an improvement.

Many Catholics are not aware of how extraordinary the lectionary given to us by the Second Vatican Council actually was. In the words of Rev. Frank C. Quinn, OP, a theologian and liturgist,

> The post-Vatican II Roman lectionary represented a profound break with the past. Not only were the readings organized according to a plan whereby a richer fare of scripture was read in liturgical celebrations, in contrast to the medieval lectionary where the choice of readings was simply helter-skelter, but for the first time in history the Sunday lectionary covered a period of three years, each year being dedicated to a particular synoptic author—Matthew, Mark or Luke. A fourth year was not dedicated to the Gospel of John because readings from this gospel permeate the sacred seasons, especially the latter part of Lent and most of Easter. Another innovation was the reintroduction of Old Testament readings into the Catholic liturgy, which had practically vanished except for such special situations as the Easter vigil and Ember Days. One result is that preachers are becoming more aware of the need to grapple with the Old Testament—which includes, for Roman Catholics, both the Hebrew and the Greek scriptures—and not just the gospel. Other changes: three readings on Sunday instead of two, a weekday lectionary that provides a one-year cycle of readings from the gospel and a two-year cycle for the first reading.[1]

The pre-Vatican II lectionary contained a handful of verses from the four major prophets—Isaiah, Jeremiah, Ezekiel, and Daniel—and only a sprinkling from the twelve Minor Prophets—Hosea , Joel, Amos, Jonah, Micah, and Zechariah. Now, however, all the prophets appear except the shortest, Obadiah. Currently, on Sundays and major feasts, selections from Isaiah appear forty-seven times, from Jeremiah and Ezekiel nine times, and from Daniel three times. It is instructive to compare the frequency of the lectionary quotations of the Old Testament with how frequently the New Testament (and Dead Sea Scrolls) quotes Old Testament books. The New Testament quotes most frequently Psalms, Isaiah, and

---

1. Frank C. Quinn, "The Roman Lectionary and the Scriptures Read in Church," *National Catholic Reporter* 31, no. 5 (November 18, 1994): 6.

Deuteronomy, in that order. Christians of that period considered David to be a prophet and hence read the psalms as if they were prophetic texts. Deuteronomy, the third most cited Old Testament book in the New Testament, does not appear in the liturgy with great frequency, only nine times in the Sunday lectionary and thirteen times in the weekday lectionary.

Today, Mass-goers on Sundays and major feasts can expect to hear a prophet as the Old Testament first reading about 50 percent of the time, and in the weekday lectionary (which has only two readings in contrast to three on Sunday), about 42 percent of the time. Unfortunately, most of the readings from the prophets are too brief to provide a context that might enable people to understand them sufficiently. Taken out of context the prophets can come across as denouncers rather than announcers, harsh critics rather than pastoral guides. In spite of this limitation, however, prophets speak so powerfully that they inevitably shape hearers' thoughts and actions.

Though we can be grateful for the increased presence of the prophets in the *Lectionary for Mass*, there is one problem, which will be addressed more fully later in this book. The lectionary editors too often chose prophetic texts to serve as a foil to the Gospel texts that were thought to "fulfill" it. Such a criterion for choosing can easily give the impression that the prophetic text can be put aside once it has exercised its function of pointing to the New Testament. Even the chapter on the Old Testament in the Second Vatican Council document *Dei Verbum* (Word of God), inevitably a product of its time, did not venture beyond this mid-twentieth century Catholic view. The consensus at that time saw the Old Testament as mainly preparatory for the New. As *Dei Verbum* (6.15) states, "These books [Old Testament], even though they contain matters imperfect and provisional, nevertheless show us authentic divine teaching." This book aims to show that the prophets not only contribute to the dynamic of the Christian Bible, but they are hugely significant on their own as thinkers and pastoral guides.

The view that the Old Testament is provisional risks making the prophets mere predictors of a distant future instead of faithful interpreters of events happening before their eyes. To take but one example, the lectionary for the Twenty-Fifth Sunday of Ordinary Time, year C, pairs Amos 8:4–7, a denunciation of those who trample on the needy ("Hear this, you who trample upon the needy"), with Luke 16:1–13, the parable of the dishonest manager. True, both speak of deceptive business practices, yet Amos vigorously chastises merchants cheating impoverished families, whereas Jesus in Luke has a more abstract goal—to recommend that his disciples bring something of the manager's shrewdness into their religious lives. Amos provides the fire missing in Luke. His condemnation of heartless exploitation has lost none of its relevance for today and his emphasis is perfectly compatible with Jesus' challenge.

Influence of the Prophets in the Prayers of the Mass

Though liturgical prayers seldom quote the Hebrew prophets, the prophets' influence on the liturgy shows up strongly in an indirect way. They inject a strong forward motion into the Christian reading of the Bible, and consequently into the way we hear liturgical readings. Thanks to the prophets, we sense that divine promises given in the past influence present events and invite Christian hearers to see themselves involved in a divinely led history. Think of Advent and Christmas Time, for example, wherein we are reminded of the fulfillment of hopes generated by "the prophets of old" (Mark 6:15, NRSV). Fulfillment in turn generates hope in the future coming of the Messiah. Think of Lent and Easter Time when the Church draws lessons for today from Israel's forty-year wilderness journey to the promised land and looks forward to further fulfillment in the resurrected life of Jesus.

Meeting the Prophets in Christian Pictorial Art

Christian art has often been displayed in churches, where it can resonate with and reinforce the viewer's experience of the Mass. It has usually devoted less attention to the prophets than to more readily imagined stories, such as Adam and Eve in the Garden of Eden, Noah and the Flood, the sacrifice of Isaac, David's battles and rise to kingship, and stories about Solomon, Samson, Tobit, Esther, and Judith.

Early Christian artists leaned heavily on typological and Christological readings of Old Testament texts—that is, interpretations of characters and events that pointed forward to the New Testament. Here are some examples: the sacrifice of Isaac is a type or figurative image of Christ, Jonah swallowed by the large fish is a type of the resurrection, and Moses receiving the tablets of the law points forward to Christ as the fulfillment of the law. Paintings from the Renaissance period and thereafter exhibit similar tendencies. This tendency comes to particularly vivid expression in the Sistine Chapel ceiling by Michelangelo (1475–1564). He made several prophets structurally significant in his design of the ceiling—Daniel, Joel, Zechariah, Jeremiah, Ezekiel, Isaiah, and Jonah. Michelangelo caught them in action, for example, painting Jeremiah lamenting the fall of Jerusalem, and Ezekiel listening intently to the word of the Lord.

In the chapel of the Boston College School of Theology and Ministry, where I teach, a remarkable series of stained-glass windows

Ezekiel, from Michaelangelo's Sistine Chapel ceiling, 1508–1512, chromolithograph by Storch and Kramer after C. Mariannecci after Michelangelo, 1871.

offers a standard Christian interpretation of the prophets. We are not sure of the artist or even of the date, though we do know the windows go back at least to 1937. As one looks toward the back of the chapel from the sanctuary, one sees that the stained-glass windows on the left wall depict Old Testament figures, and those on the right their New Testament counterparts.

In the first window, beneath a shepherd's staff is John the Baptist (belonging to the Old Testament) holding a shell to pour water on those whom he baptizes. Opposite him on the right, similarly equipped with a shepherd's staff, is Saint Joseph (New Testament) with a dove above him descending like the Holy Spirit.

The next window on the left depicts the priest Melchizedek with the bread and wine he brought out to celebrate the victorious Abraham (Genesis 14). Opposite is *Christus sacerdos*, "Christ the priest," holding a cup of wine, symbol of the Eucharist.

In the third window, a bearded and grave Moses holds twin tablets on which are written the Ten Commandments. Opposite Moses in the right window is Jesus declaring *Ego sum vobiscum*, "I am with you" (refer to Matthew 1:23 and 28:20), evidently meant to complement the depiction of Moses holding the daunting Ten Commandments.

Fourth, next to last on the left, a beardless and youthful Isaiah holds a placard with words from the suffering servant song in Isaiah 53, *livore ejus sanati sumus*, "by his wounds we are healed." Opposite these words uttered by the suffering Isaian servant is a suffering Jesus with the title *Christus victima*, "Christ the victim."

The final window on the left shows a beardless Daniel writing in a book, apparently his visions of the eternal kingdom replacing the kingdoms of the world (Daniel 2 and 7). Opposite Daniel is *Christus rex*, "Christ the king," exercising the eternal kingship bestowed on the Son of Man by the Ancient of Days in Daniel 7.

We must interpret the left and the right stained glass windows correctly. Yes, the right wall illustrates the trajectory of the events sketched on the left wall. In no way, however, do the opposite pictures reduce earlier events to mere predictions. The events depicted on the right wall, we need to remember, have their own inherent trajectory or forward motion. They too will be "fulfilled" in the sense that the Holy Spirit will provide a fuller understanding of the New Testament events for Christians: the Eucharist will become a heavenly banquet that will satisfy guests' deepest needs. Christ's promise to be with the Church will be fulfilled in a variety of ways. Christ the servant's sufferings will bring about salvation, and Christ will indeed exercise universal kingship. In short, the Spirit-led dynamic revealed in the left-right movement in the windows does not end even with the right window. Both panels display the ongoing presence-in-action of the Living God.

Meeting the Prophets in Christian Hymns

Christian hymns also show the influence of the Old Testament prophets. The people's response in the Preface of the Mass, "Holy, Holy, Holy," is based on the heavenly choir's song in Isaiah 6:2-5: "Seraphim were stationed above; each of them had six wings: with two they covered their faces, with two they covered their feet, and with two they hovered. One cried out to the other: 'Holy, holy, holy is the LORD of hosts! All the earth is filled with his glory!'"[2] The beautiful Advent hymn "O Come, O Come, Emanuel" is derived from Isaiah 7:14, "Therefore the Lord himself will give you this sign: the virgin shall conceive and bear a son, and shall name him Emmanuel."[3] John W. Work's spiritual, "Go, tell it on the mountain, over the hills and everywhere; go, tell it on the mountain that Jesus Christ is born" restates Isaiah 40:9, "'Go up onto a high mountain, / Zion, herald of glad tidings, / cry out at the top of your voice, / Jerusalem, herald of

---

2. Heard on the Saturday of the Fourteenth Week in Ordinary Time, year 2, and partially on the Fifth Sunday in Ordinary Time, year C.

3. Heard on the Fourth Sunday of Advent, year A.

good news! / Fear not to cry out / and say to the cities of Judah: / Here is your God!"[4]

Both Mark 1:3 and John 1:23 describe John the Baptist echoing Isaiah 40:3, "In the desert prepare the way of the LORD!" which influenced the Lenten hymn "On Jordan's bank the Baptist's cry announces that the Lord is nigh. Awake and harken, for he brings glad tidings of the King of kings!" Ezekiel's vision of scattered Israel as dry bones gradually joining into living beings in chapter 37 has shaped the spiritual "Dry Bones" an exceptionally literal borrowing from the prophets.

The 1949 hymn by Alfred F. Bayly "What Does the Lord Require" is taken from Micah 6:8, while Daniel 7, in which the Ancient of Days granted eternal kingships to the Son of man has inspired several hymns: "Ancient of Days," by William Croswell Doane, 1886, "Lo, He Comes with Clouds Descending," by Charles Wesley, 1758, and the hymn text "Come, Thou Almighty King," (unknown author), often sung to the hymn tune ITALIAN HYMN, composed by Felice de Giardini in the eighteenth century. This hymn text is very well known: "Come, Thou Almighty King, help us Thy name to sing, help us to praise. Father, all glorious, o'er all victorious, come, and reign over us, Ancient of Days." A 1982 hymn by Michael Joncas, "A Voice Cries Out," is based on Isaiah 40:1–11.

By now, it should be clear that appreciating the prophets in the liturgy, "hearing" them in the fullest sense, involves more than hearing them read in church. We gain our knowledge of them in bits and pieces, through interpretation. Interpretation is a concept many of us hardly ever speak about and quite often misunderstand. It is time to say something about it.

---

4. Heard on the Second Sunday of Advent, year B, and on the Feast of the Baptism of the Lord, year C.

The Challenge of Interpreting the Prophets

At this point, readers may be disappointed that I have not yet spoken directly about the Hebrew prophets themselves and how New Testament authors understood them, but instead have talked about how later writers and artists "heard" them. The time for speaking about the prophets themselves will come soon enough and in fact will constitute the major part of the book. But first we must deal with a neglected but necessary topic—the interpretation of the Bible. It is necessary, but discussion of it is often neglected.

What I have said in the previous paragraphs about the lectionary's selections from the prophets rests on the issue of interpretation. The *Lectionary for Mass* is itself a work of interpretation. Its designers have engaged in interpretation by selecting certain prophetic texts and not selecting others. The old lectionary interpreted the prophets by paying them little heed. The revised lectionary interprets the prophets by including them and giving them a major place. Michelangelo interpreted them by portraying them as part of the Christian firmament. Hymn composers took this or that verse from the prophets and developed them in their own way. The architect of my school's chapel interpreted the prophets relationally—that is, defining them largely by their relation to New Testament figures.

All of these instances are interpretations of the prophets. We moderns often grow impatient with interpretation. We might dismiss it as someone else's perspective, not our own. Do away with the middle man! We like things straightforward, unvarnished, without spin. Why waste time on others' viewpoints? But such a desire for direct and unmediated contact, for "authenticity" without interpretation, is a delusion. Facts don't enter immediately into our brain. As we see an event, we interpret it in the very moment we see it taking place. Is that gunshot we heard in the night a backfiring car, a neighbor setting off fireworks, or a terrorist's gun? Is the stranger approaching me with his head down friendly or hostile? Is the book I am reading truthful or misleading?

Though we may not think about it often, both Judaism and Christianity over the centuries developed rules and traditions for interpreting the Scriptures, including the prophets. As the former Chief Rabbi of the Commonwealth[5] Jonathan Sacks puts it, "The rabbis said, 'One who translates a verse literally is a liar.' The point is clear. No text without interpretation; no interpretation without tradition."[6] On the Christian side, Robert Louis Wilkin states succinctly the interpretive framework with which the Church fathers read their Bible: "The church fathers were no less aware than we that the books of the Bible come from disparate authors and different historical periods. Yet the Scriptures they sought to understand was a single book, and all its tributaries and rivulets flowed into the great river of God's revelation, the creation of the world, the history of Israel, the life of Christ and the beginning of the church, the final vision of the heavenly city. . . . Exegesis was theological, and theology was exegetical."[7]

The following pages view the prophets as Christian Scripture, *interpreted in the Christian tradition.* Hearing the prophets in a tradition does not mean hearing them prepackaged. One hears them as part of a tradition that does not end with them, but continues in their successors—in particular, in the tradition of Jesus the prophet. Far from being strait-jacketed, interpretation flourishes within a tradition. Speaking within a tradition means that others will understand us and respond to us. Interpreting the prophets

---

5. The Commonwealth of Nations, consisting principally of nations that were former territories of the United Kingdom.

6. I borrow from my article "What the Biblical Scribes Teach Us about Their Writings," *Theological Studies* 79, no. 3 (2018): 654. The Sachs quote is in *Not in God's Name: Confronting Religious Violence* (New York: Schocken Books, 2015), 208. The quotation is from the Babylonian Talmud, Kiddushin, 49a.

7. Robert Louis Wilkin, *The Spirit of Early Christian Thought* (New Haven, CT: Yale University Press, 2003), 314–15. Two words in the above quote may require comment. *Exegesis* means "explanation" or "exposition" of a literary passage, and it is often used by biblical scholars. It is derived from two ancient Greek words meaning "to lead" and "out"—that is, to lead or bring out the meaning of a passage. *Theology* refers to the study of religious faith, especially of God and God's relation to the world. It also is derived from two Greek words meaning "God" and "word, explanation."

within the Christian tradition means not neglecting Jewish viewpoints. On the contrary, on most points of interpretation about the prophets, Christians and Jews usually agree.

An example of agreement between Christians and Jews is the prophets' insistence on social justice. Judaism has a long and enviable record of championing human rights, not just for Jews, but for all human beings, one reason being that Genesis 1:27 made clear that every human is created in the image of God: "So God created humankind in his image, in the image of God he created them; male and female he created them." The prophets preached consistently the implications of that central truth. Christians and Jews will disagree, however, on what the prophets foresaw in the far future. Jews tend to view the prophets as interpreters of the Torah (Pentateuch) and speaking to the situation in front of them—what was happening to the people in their lifetime. Christian interpreters would not deny that the writing prophets were primarily addressing their contemporary situation, but they would insist that God was hinting at a future that would yet unfold. To Christians, that future involved Jesus, the Son of God.

The prophets are not always a preparation for the New Testament. They have an authority and beauty of their own.

One of the most important sources of interpretation for most Christians is the *Lectionary for Mass*, for it places prophetic texts in the context of more familiar New Testament texts. Christians seldom hear (and alas, seldom read) the prophets by themselves. Usually we hear them read aloud with other biblical passages. Hearing them in the liturgy provides a wonderfully rich context, though it can, unless we are aware, distort our view of the prophets, for they are not always a preparation for the New Testament. Not exclusively preparatory and predictive, the prophets have an authority and beauty of their own. How to resolve the two perspectives of "predictive" and "authoritative-on-their-own" will occupy us in the last section of this book.

CHAPTER 2

Prophets in the Ancient Near East and Prophets in the Bible: Abraham to Elisha

Prophets in the Ancient Near East

Only a few decades ago scholars assumed that the Hebrew prophets were unique in the ancient Near East. There was nothing like them in the ancient world! Neighboring peoples might have literature similar to Israel's historical narratives, laws, and wisdom literature, but surely there were no parallels to the Hebrew prophets who fearlessly preached worship of YHWH alone, spoke boldly to the king, and insisted on strict social justice. "Yahweh" is the probable name of Israel's God in the Old Testament. Even before the New Testament, however, Jews considered it too sacred to pronounce and used "the Lord" instead. Christians followed suit. Jews, along with many Christians today, write the name using only the consonants YHWH.

Two discoveries in recent years have shaken that comforting assumption. The first was the unearthing over the past few decades of dozens of prophetic oracles and texts describing their use. Many of the texts were composed in the second-millennium BC city of Mari in today's eastern Syria. Another group were prophecies excavated at Nineveh, one of the capitals of the Neo-Assyrian Empire (935–612 BC; today Iraq). These and texts like them demonstrated that prophecy similar to the Israelite phenomenon was practiced in other Near Eastern cultures. Of course, the biblical prophets were not exactly like those of Israel's neighbors—we will come to the Israelite difference later—but there were important similarities, which detract not in the least from the Bible or from their neighbors' literature. In short, the prophetic texts in the Bible were not unique in the ancient world.

The second "discovery" was less a discovery and more a reappraisal of the context of prophecy—divination and magic. Though divination and magic were practiced everywhere in the

The prophetic texts in the Bible were not unique in the ancient world.

ancient Near East, biblical scholars were accustomed to write off such phenomena as little more than superstitious attempts to control the future. Recent scholarship, however, has begun to see matters differently. This second look appreciates divination as a rational and painstaking method to gain divine knowledge about the future that was not otherwise available to human beings. Moreover, modern scholarship interprets "magic," normally a pejorative term among biblical scholars, to be in many circumstances careful attempts to cooperate with the divine intent regarding human history. We should keep in mind that ancient people believed in divine causality in much the same way that we moderns believe, say, in the laws of physics—gravity, electricity, motion, and the like.

The beliefs concerning divine causality did not necessarily make them pious, but they at least made ancient people realistic about the limits of humans' role in the world. The ancients' wariness led them to develop a variety of methods for gaining knowledge essential for interpreting current events and caring for their crops and herds. It was especially important to understand the weather and climate, for ancient economies were largely based on agriculture. Unforeseen climate change could bring disaster.

It is wise, then, to interpret the prophets as not unique to Israel or limited to Canaan, but rather as individuals engaging in a widespread ancient Near Eastern practice of "divination" and "magic," though, we must emphasize, they prophesied in a uniquely biblical way. Divination must be understood broadly. "The diviner," in the words of Martti Nissinen of the University of Helsinki and a pioneer in widening our perspective, was "an intermediary between the human and superhuman domains and [expert at using] a considerable variety of methods of divination. These methods are often divided into two broad categories: (1) technical, or *inductive*,[1] methods that involve systematization of signs and omens by observing physical objects (extispicy [the reading of animal entrails], astrology, lot-casting, bird, fish, and oil divination, etc.); and (2) *intuitive*, or *inspired*, or *non-inductive* methods, such as dreams, visions, and, [of special interest to us] prophecy."[2] We will focus on the second category—intuitive, or inspired, or non-inductive methods—of acquiring "the secrets of the gods." To attain this end in the world of the Bible, the chief means was prophecy.

Prophets in Israel

The Three Clusters of Prophetic Texts in the Old Testament

Within the Bible, prophetic narratives and oracles appear mainly in three clusters of texts—(1) stories about the emergence of kingship in the eleventh and tenth centuries BC (the books of Samuel-Kings), (2) ninth-century stories about the prophets Elijah and Elisha (1 Kings 17–2 Kings 13); and (3) the prophetic books themselves (the third part of the Christian Bible and the Latter Prophets in the Jewish Bible). The prophetic books record events that took place around 750–500 BC, though they were edited and published later. Prior to the first cluster in Samuel-Kings, however, the designation "prophet" was given to individuals known for their access to heavenly knowledge, notably Abraham (Genesis 20:7) and Moses (Deuteronomy18:15).

---

1. An inductive method draws a conclusion from specific evidence.

2. I am indebted here to Martti Nissinen, *Ancient Prophecy: Near Eastern, Biblical, and Greek Perspectives* (Oxford: Oxford University Press, 2017), 14–15. Italics mine.

Where Do the Prophets Fit in the Christian Bible?

New Testament authors regarded "the Law and the Prophets" (one of their terms for the Scriptures) as the indispensable first part of a longer narrative that continued right up to their own day. The New Testament view becomes clear if we compare the Christian "Old Testament" to the Jewish Bible, called Tanakh. Both Tanakh and the Old Testament have three sections. ("Old Testament" comes into use for the Scriptures only in the late second century AD.) Tanakh consists of a core—the Torah (Pentateuch)—around which are placed the Prophets, Former and Latter ("Former" refers to Joshua to Kings, and "Latter" to the Major and Minor Prophets, minus Daniel). In the Tanakh arrangement, the prophets illustrate or explicate the Torah. The third section of Tanakh, the Writings (the remaining books) are in less direct ways also oriented to the Torah in the center. Tanakh's arrangement emphasizes God's election of Israel and gift to them of his authoritative and community-forming instruction given at Sinai through Moses. Though Tanakh has an orientation to the future (evidenced among other signs by the Jewish concept of "the world to come"), it does not envision the future with the concreteness and particularity of the New Testament, nor does it see itself as the first act of a two-act scenario.

The Christian Bible, on the other hand, sees the ancient Scriptures as the first act of a two-act story. By placing all the historical books in its first section, the ancient editors invite readers to view the Pentateuch as the beginning of a story that will continue in the books of Joshua to Kings, Ezra to Nehemiah, Chronicles, and (in the Catholic and Orthodox canon) 1 and 2 Maccabees of the second and first centuries BC. The last of its three sections are the prophetic books, which form a doorway to the New Testament. Malachi, the last prophet, is followed immediately by the Gospel of Matthew. The prophets in the Old Testament become to some extent "foretellers" (of Christ), though Christians deeply appreciate along with their Jewish neighbors the prophets' foretelling the promises and demands of Torah.

"Prophets" Prior to the Writing Prophets

I have suggested viewing the Old Testament prophets under the broad category of "divination," in which a prophet was defined as an intermediary revealing to humans the hidden knowledge of the gods. With this definition, it is not surprising that the term *prophet* was applied loosely to some early Israelite intermediaries. Genesis 20:7, for example, calls Abraham a prophet. God tells Abimelech, "So now, return the man's wife [Sarah] so that he may intercede for you, since [Abraham] is a prophet, that you may live. If you do not return her, you can be sure that you and all who are yours will die." Note that the excerpt assumes that intercession is part of the prophet's job description. Other books of the Pentateuch and the books of Joshua and Judges applied the term *prophet* to anyone who spoke for another, such as Aaron who spoke for his brother Moses (Exodus 7:1). It was applied to spirit-filled intermediaries (Exodus 15:20; Numbers 11:29) and indeed to any recognized speaker for Israel's God (Judges 4:4; 6:8; Deuteronomy 13:1–5). Moses bestrides the narrow world of the Old Testament like a colossus and it is not surprising that Deuteronomy portrays him as *the* prophet, for at Mount Sinai he mediates the relationship between YHWH and his people that later prophets will oversee and interpret. Deuteronomy 34:10–12 applies the term to him in a memorable eulogy at his death: "Since then no prophet has arisen in Israel like Moses, whom the Lord knew face to face, in all the signs and wonders the Lord sent him to perform in the land of Egypt against Pharaoh and all his servants and against all his land, and all the great might and the awesome power that Moses displayed in the sight of all Israel."

So "prophetic" was Moses in mediating between the people and the Lord at Israel's foundation that scholars sometimes speak of a Mosaic "office," a recognized position that continued after Moses' death. According to Deuteronomy 18:15–22, "A prophet like me will the Lord, your God, raise up for you from among your own kindred; that is the one to whom you shall listen. . . . [I] will put my words into the mouth of the prophet; the prophet shall tell them all that

I command." Centuries later, Jeremiah presumed he spoke in accord with this office when he replied to God's commission in terms similar to Moses' reply in Exodus 3:11, 13; 4:10: "'Ah, Lord God!' I said, / 'I do not know how to speak. I am too young!' / But the Lord answered me, / Do not say, 'I am too young.' / To whomever I send you, you shall go; / whatever I command you, you shall speak" (Jeremiah 1:6–7). In some circles, the Mosaic office continued to be exercised by those commissioned to oversee and strengthen Israel's relationship to the Lord. Like Moses, Jeremiah encouraged faithfulness to the covenant and excoriated infidelity; Jeremiah himself became a model servant of the Lord, which he expressed among other places through his famous "confessions" in chapters 12–20. In the New Testament, the Transfiguration alludes to the Mosaic office, "behold, a bright cloud cast a shadow over them, then from the cloud came a voice that said, 'This is my beloved Son, with whom I am well pleased; *listen* to him'" (Matthew 17:5; compare with Deuteronomy 18:15, "you shall *listen* to the prophet"—author's translation).

First Cluster of Prophetic Texts in the Bible:
The Emergence of Kingship: Samuel, Saul, and David

It was only with the emergence of kingship in the late eleventh century BC that prophets in the Bible appear in the recognizable role they will continue to exercise in the future. In the Bible, the prophets typically appear in moments of crisis when their words or actions are needed. The books of Joshua and Judges hardly mention prophets during the thirteenth-century BC conquest of Canaan and subsequent rule by tribal chieftains (called "judges" in most English translations). The only named prophet mentioned in these books is Deborah in Judges 4:4, who sits under a palm tree "where the Israelites came up to her for judgment" (Judges 4:5). Evidently, she was shrewd and prestigious enough to order the general Barak to march into battle while she drew out Sisera and his army into an area where she could deliver them into Barak's forces. There is also the unidentified "prophet" in Judges 6:8 who rebuked the people in a Moses-like way for abandoning the Lord.

The book of Samuel, on the other hand, situates prophets in the transition from rule by judges to rule by a king, which occurred in the late eleventh and early tenth centuries BC. Rule by the judges, according to the assessment of the book of Judges itself, proved unsuccessful; it brought internal chaos and violence, described with special vividness in Judges 17–21. In addition, as if Israel's internal failures were not enough, the Philistines, united under the king of Gath in the eleventh century, attacked and conquered Israel around 1050 BC. Samuel, the last of the judges, failed to free Israel from the Philistines. Forced finally to institute a permanent leader rather than waiting for regional leaders to emerge in crises, Samuel saw the need for kingship even though there was a strong Israelite tradition against kings. Despite some opposition and his own misgivings, he anointed Saul as king around 1020 BC. Initially, Saul's kingship was a limited one compared with kings in neighboring nations. In Israel, a less authoritative term, Hebrew *nāgîd*, "military commander," was used rather than the regular Hebrew word initially used for king, *melek*. Another limit on kingship was the institution of the prophet (Hebrew *nābî'*), seemingly as a check and balance to royal power. 1 Samuel portrays Samuel as the first of this kind of prophet (1 Samuel 3:20; 9:9). Samuel exercised the role of prophet as both an authorizer and critic of kingship. That "Samuel-Saul compromise" lasted as long as kingship lasted, at least according to the Deuteronomistic historians who edited the books of Joshua to Kings. The term "Deuteronomistic historians" refers to the scribes who arranged the books of Joshua, Judges, Samuel, and Kings into a coherent narrative somewhat in the spirit of the book of Deuteronomy. These scribes probably did their collecting and editing in the late seventh century (when Josiah was king, 640–609 BC) and again a generation later.

The first book of Samuel also mentions charismatic bands of "prophets" (1 Samuel, 10:5, 10–11; 19:20). It is unclear how Samuel, also called a prophet, related to such groups.

In the course of time, the relationship between Samuel and Saul deteriorated, in large measure because of the tension between human kingships (which in the ancient Near East had few restraints) and divine kingship represented by the prophet.

Samuel performed in a public way three prophetic functions that later prophets would also perform. First, he validated God's choice of Saul when God told him, "At this time tomorrow I will send you a man from the land of Benjamin whom you are to anoint as ruler of my people Israel" (1 Samuel 9:16). Samuel privately anointed Saul, and later presented him to the gathered tribes, "'Do you see the man whom the Lord has chosen? There is no one like him among all the people!' Then all the people shouted out, 'Long live the king!'" (1 Samuel 10:24). In 1 Samuel 12, Samuel articulated a "theology of kingship," upbraiding the people for opting for a king instead of trusting in their divine king. Samuel soberly insisted to them that the king is as much subject to the ancient covenant as anyone else. But just as the prophet could anoint a king, so could he reject him. In two episodes, 1 Samuel 13 and 15, Samuel rejected Saul for disobeying his commands regarding holy war, though the text raises questions about Samuel's own motivations in the rejection.

Following the example of Samuel's willingness to stand over against the king, the ninth-century prophets Elijah and Elisha involved themselves in the political life of the nation and felt free to criticize the king (1 Kings 17—2 Kings 2; 2 Kings 6–13). In the eighth and seventh centuries, Amos, Isaiah, and Jeremiah gave critiques of the king, sometimes positive, at other times negative. All the prophets in fact felt authorized by God to demand that the king and his officers, no less than the people, obey the Word of God in contrast to neighboring cultures in which royal power went virtually unchecked.

Samuel exercised a third function that prophets later emulated —speaking up for the ancient traditions rooted in the formation of the people under Moses. At Sinai, the people who had just been freed from the pharaoh's tyranny accepted the Lord's invitation to be his people (Exodus 19:3–6). They promised absolute fidelity to the LORD, accepted his gifts, and in doing so became a people with a common god (and temple), land, leader, and defining legal and narrative traditions. The prophets' task was to remind king and people to live in accord with the covenantal relationship and to care for "the widow and orphan," an ancient phrase used throughout the ancient Near East to describe the most vulnerable members of society. Widows and orphans were vulnerable because they were without the protection that a large family would have provided.

After anointing David as king in 1 Samuel 16, Samuel largely drops out of the story except in chapters 19 and 28. The next prophet to play a prominent role in relation to the king was one of David's own court prophets, Nathan. He figures in three important episodes. In 2 Samuel 7, which records God's promise to David that his dynasty would be eternal, David asks Nathan to inquire about his plan to build a palace for the Lord. The Lord was housed in a tent, a traditional dwelling for a god, though evidently insignificant compared to a royal palace. As might be expected of a court prophet, Nathan at first told David to follow his heart and build a house for the Lord.

> But that same night the word of the Lord came to Nathan: Go and tell David my servant. Thus says the Lord: Is it you who would build me a house to dwell in? I have never dwelt in a house from the day I brought Israel up from Egypt to this day, but I have been going about in a tent or a tabernacle. As long as I have wandered about among the Israelites, did I ever say a word to any of the judges whom I commanded to shepherd my people Israel: Why have you not built me a house of cedar? Now then, speak thus to my servant David, Thus says the Lord of hosts: the Lord also declares to you that the Lord will make you a house.
> (2 Samuel 7:4–8a, 11c)

The oracle contains a wordplay on "house." I will build you a house (dynasty), you will not build me a house (temple).

On the Fourth Sunday of Advent, year B, 2 Samuel 7 is paired with Luke 1:25–38. Listeners move from the royal court in Jerusalem where David seeks to build a house for the Lord to Mary's humble dwelling in Nazareth where she herself will become a "house" for the Lord. The juxtaposition shows the unexpected ways by which God's word is fulfilled.

Nathan later showed his mettle when he condemned David for his adultery with Bathsheba and murder of her husband Uriah in 2 Samuel 12. Knowing how difficult it was for a court prophet, a royal employee, to condemn a king, Nathan took an indirect route to call out the king for committing adultery with Uriah's wife Bathsheba and devising the murder of his loyal servant Uriah. To prepare the king to repent, Nathan told him a parable about a rich man who seized a poor neighbor's prized lamb, a family pet, to feed an important guest, instead of taking an animal from his own flocks. On hearing Nathan's story, David flew into a rage and declared the man deserved to die and should repay the poor man fourfold. Having disarmed David by his parable, Nathan declared, "That man is you!" (2 Samuel 12:7). The parable had its desired effect. David repented, though he still had to endure the awful consequences of his sin—a murder within his own family and the near loss of his throne when his own son Absalom led a rebellion against him. The story of Nathan's parable and David's repentance is found in the lectionary reading for the Third Week in Ordinary Time, Saturday, year 2, and is matched with Mark 4:35–41, Jesus' calming of the storm and the disciples' awe of the one whom even wind and sea obey. How the readings illuminate each other is not obvious. Maybe a contrast is intended between David admitting his guilt, and yet forced to live with the dreadful consequences, whereas the disciples in Mark experience terror but are rescued when they ask Jesus' help.

In his last appearance, in 1 Kings 1, Nathan inserted himself into court politics regarding David's successor, Solomon. Aligning himself with the party of Zakok, the priest, and David's elite warriors, he persuaded Solomon's mother Bathsheba to lobby for her son Solomon against David's oldest son Adonijah. Nathan was successful. The elderly and failing David summoned up his energy to support Solomon rather than his eldest son Adonijah (1 Kings 1).

The other court prophet, Gad, appears in the aftermath of David's ill-advised attempt to take a census of the people in 2 Samuel 24. Gad relays to the king the three options God decrees as punishment: three years of famine, three months of fleeing from his enemy, or three days of plague. David chose the last punishment. When the plague stopped unexpectedly, Gad directed David to set up an altar to the Lord on the threshing floor of Araunah the Jebusite.

After the split of the Northern and Southern Kingdoms around 922 BC, a northern prophet, Ahijah, announced to Jeroboam, leader of the rebellion, that YHWH would grant to him rule over ten tribes, leaving Solomon and the house of David only Judah (1 Kings 11:26–40).

Second Cluster of Prophetic Stories: Elijah and Elisha in the Ninth Century

The second cluster of prophetic texts comes a century after David ruled, when two prophets suddenly appear, Elijah and Elisha. The political situation had changed since David. By around 930 BC in Israel, toward the end of Solomon's reign, two polities ruled by kings had developed, Judah with its center in Jerusalem, and the wealthier and more populous Israel, including the hill country of Ephraim and centered on Shechem and Gilead. ("Israel" is an ambiguous term, referring at times to the Northern Kingdom and at other times to the entire nation, Judah and Israel.) It was not until the ninth century, however, that Omri, a shrewd king, brought stability and renown to the Northern Kingdom (876–842 BC). Renewing an alliance with Tyre, he arranged a dynastic marriage of Jezebel, the daughter of the Tyrian king Ittobaal, to the crown prince, Ahab. Omri's son Ahab was the first king of Israel to face an expansionistic Assyria under Shalmaneser III. One of his achievements was to join with the kings of Damascus and Hamath to stop Assyria in the battle of Qarqar in 853 BC. He was less successful in his domestic policies. His queen, Jezebel, who brought with her the gods she had revered in Tyre, vigorously sponsored the worship of Baal of Tyre, presumably Melqart, the god of the royal house, a storm god. According to 1 Kings 16:31–34,

Ahab built an altar to Baal in the temple of Baal. An annual "awakening" of Melqart was celebrated at Tyre and elsewhere in the presence of the king from the tenth century BC, which may be relevant to the contest of Baal versus YHWH in 1 Kings 18:25–39.

Elijah had no doubts about the primacy of YHWH; no other god could be worshiped. His name meant "My God (*Eli-*) is YHWH (*Jah*)." Originally from Gilead, east of the Jordan River, Elijah vigorously combatted the syncretistic worship practiced by the royal house. Ahab probably included YHWH among the gods he worshiped, but evidently gave greater prominence to Baal of Tyre. In his very first appearance (1 Kings 17:1), Elijah called down a three-year drought upon Israel showing dramatically what deity controlled life-giving rain. At God's command, he then went to Zarephath, deep in Phoenician territory, the bailiwick of Jezebel, where he restored life to the son of the widow who hosted him, showing that God has the power to give life even in Phoenicia. YHWH's power to provide rain and give life—gifts proper to the god of storm—will be a major topic of the following stories. 1 Kings 17:1–16 and 17–24 appears on Monday and Tuesday of the Tenth Week, year 2. The two readings are paired with excerpts from Matthew's Sermon on the Mount, Matthew 5:1–12 and 13–16. The continuity of the Gospel texts suggests there is no thematic connection between the Old and the New Testament readings. Listeners can interpret Matthew's beatitudes as guides for the life God wishes us to live. The Old Testament reading tells how Elijah announced that God was withholding life-giving rain, yet fed the prophet, demonstrating God's total control over life.

1 Kings 18 is an exciting contest between the prophets of Baal and the lone prophet of YHWH, Elijah. Elijah succeeds in calling down drought-ending rain by invoking the Lord, whereas the dancing and self-slashing of the four hundred prophets of Baal achieve nothing. Having defeated the prophets of Baal, Elijah commands that the Baal prophets be slaughtered. Elijah tells the defeated King Ahab to return to his royal residence in Jezreel. "But the hand of the Lord was on Elijah; he girded up his clothing and ran before Ahab as far as

the approaches to Jezreel" (1 Kings 18:46). As any reader instinctively surmises, the stories of Elijah and Elisha are prophetic legends. Their historicity will be discussed at the conclusion of the Elisha stories.

In another memorable episode (1 Kings 19), Elijah, exhausted and fleeing from Jezebel's wrath, returns to the source of Israel's covenant, Sinai (called Horeb in this account) where he has an encounter with YHWH reminiscent of Moses' encounter. This time the meeting is unlike the first. The Lord does not appear in wind, earthquake, and fire, but in "a light silent sound" (I Kings 19:12), a phrase that puzzles commentators. Perhaps it is a verbal assurance validating the prophet's ministry, a rejection of the traditional storm accompaniments of Melqart of Tyre, or an affirmation of the ministry of Elijah. "A light silent sound" does not mean a gentle relationship, however, for God gives the prophet three tasks that involve violence and revolution: anoint Hazael as king over Aram (showing the Lord's authority over a foreign nation), anoint Jehu (who will lead a bloody revolt) over Israel, and anoint Elisha "as prophet to succeed you" (1 Kings 19:16).

The stories of Elijah and Elisha are prophetic legends.

Elijah's meeting with God is the first reading on the Nineteenth Sunday in Ordinary Time, year A, where it accompanies Matthew 14:22–33, Jesus walking on the water and Peter sinking in it. Peter sinks because he fears the wind and the water. "Immediately, Jesus stretched out his hand and caught Peter, and said to him, 'O you of little faith, why did you doubt?' Awed by wind and water, Peter did not recognize "a tiny whispering sound," the presence of Jesus.

In another episode (1 Kings 21), Elijah speaks up for social justice, in the form of land tenure traditions. Elijah rebukes King Ahab for forcibly taking the land of Naboth, a peasant, and having him killed. The episode shows Elijah exercising the prophetic role of defending ancient legal traditions, specifically the tradition that the land belonged ultimately to the Lord and was meant to remain in a family; no individual family member could alienate such property.

Not even a king could annul this tradition. Ahab initially recognizes the validity of the farmer, Naboth, not to sell his property to the king. But Jezebel, who cared nothing for such traditions, assured Ahab that she would take care of Naboth. She had him killed, which invited Elijah to pronounce a sentence of death upon her, a sentence that eventually came to pass many years later.

In a dramatic finale to his life (2 Kings 2:1–18), Elijah is taken up to heaven. He and his devoted successor, Elisha, know the time is near. "As they walked on still conversing, a fiery chariot and fiery horses came between the two of them, and Elijah went up to heaven in a whirlwind" (2 Kings 2:11). Since Elijah was taken up to heaven, he became in later literature a figure like Enoch, who also was taken up (Genesis 5:23) and could therefore appear on earth to announce divine plans, as in Malachi 3:23–24, Mark 9:11–13, and often in the New Testament. As Elijah is about to be taken up, his disciple Elisha asks for a double share of his spirit. When Elisha picked up the mantle that had fallen from Elijah, he used it to strike the waters of the Jordan and saw the river parting, a sign that Elijah's gift had passed on to Elisha. The episode authenticates Elisha and associates both prophets with the exodus and Moses. Recall Deuteronomy 18:15: "A prophet like me will the LORD your God raise up for you from among your own kindred."

Elisha succeeds Elijah as prophet. 1 Kings 2–13 contains three sets of stories about him. In the first set, Elisha wins recognition as the legitimate successor to Elijah (2 Kings 2:8–18) and then becomes involved in Israel's war with neighboring Moab. The second set (2 Kings 4–5) portrays Elisha as a miracle worker in stories that resemble the *Fioretti di San Francesco* (*The Little Flowers of St. Francis*), fifty-four short chapters about the marvelous adventures of St. Francis. Some of the Elisha stories echo those about Elijah: 2 Kings 4:1–8 (compare this with 1 Kings 17:8–16) and 2 Kings 4:8–37 (compare with 1 Kings 17:17–24). One lengthy story, 2 Kings 5, is a literary masterpiece, detailing Elisha's encounter with Naaman, the powerful Syrian general who has to learn humility from Elisha before he can be cured. It may once have been a miracle story, but it has been reshaped to underline Naaman's conversion when he acknowledges the unrivaled power of Israel's God. In the last of the three sets of stories (2 Kings 6–7), Elisha retrieves an ax head that had fallen into a well. A lengthy narrative follows that combines two stories, one of Elisha's gracious treatment of captured Aramaeans and the other of the Aramaeans' cruel treatment of the inhabitants of Samaria. The next to last story about Elisha (2 Kings 8) returns to the Shunammite woman (2 Kings 4:8–37) which, some scholars have suggested, contains a subtle critique of prophets as chiefly healers and miracle workers, favoring instead book-and-word-prophets like Jeremiah and Ezekiel. The Elisha cycle climaxes with Elisha anointing Jehu, thereby starting the revolution that ended the Omride dynasty (2 Kings 9). The story of Elisha's death is found in 2 Kings 13:14–21.

The lectionary often pairs the miracle stories involving Elisha with the miracles performed by Jesus. There are several reasons for this. The evangelists wanted to demonstrate Jesus' credentials as an authentic prophet by shaping narratives about him that evoked the great wonder workers, Elijah and Elisha. Jesus did what they did, often in grander fashion. Therefore, God endorses him. Evoking Elisha also helped to demonstrate that Jesus also helped people in simple ways, like Elisha retrieving an ax head for a man who had borrowed it (2 Kings 6:5–7). Most of the miracles worked by Elijah and Elisha, however, showed God's mastery of life, whether bestowing rain or withholding it, healing illnesses, or raising the dead.

It should be clear by now that the Elijah and Elisha stories are not history as we understand it today. Most moderns are comfortable with the much-quoted definition of the great German historian Leopold van Ranke (who died in 1886): "[History] seeks only to show the past as it really was (*wie es eigentlich gewesen*)." The Dutch cultural historian Johan Huizinga (died 1945) comes closer to biblical usage: "History is the intellectual form in which a civilization renders account to itself of its past." Though modern readers sometimes balk at taking biblical stories as historical, biblical scribes firmly believed they were writing history, for like historians today, they intended to give an account of the past for their own generation. But, importantly, they did it their way. They interpreted the past by composing narratives, but narratives of a certain type. It's helpful here to consider the literary genre of legend.

Though the scholarly definition of legend is debated, and scholars struggle to distinguish the legend genre from the genres of folktale and myth, it is common to define legend as a narrative whose content and structure emphasize the virtue of the protagonist.

The following homely comparison may help us understand this biblical mode of writing history more clearly than a detailed discussion of genre. In describing an event, we today are "two-paragraph writers," that is, we describe the event "objectively" in the first paragraph, and in the second, give our interpretation. For example, we might describe a sudden cure of a serious cancer by detailing the disease in the first paragraph, and in a second paragraph listing the interpretations of physicians, family members, and religious authorities. Biblical scribes, however, faced with an extraordinary event, composed the story to highlight the wondrous element in order that God be praised, and people be instructed in the right path. Scribes added, highlighted, or omitted narrative details to achieve those purposes. Such history writing frustrates modern historians who want to get at the facts, at "what actually happened." But modern historians cannot go behind the interpretation of a biblical story, for the interpretation is woven into the biblical narrative. The story itself *is* the interpretation. Moderns who brand such writings with condescending terms like "unhistorical" or "theological fiction" only show their inability to understand this kind of history writing.[3]

The lectionary has selected the more dramatic Elijah stories—his fleeing King Ahab, his stay with the widow of Zarephath, and the cure of her son (all in 1 Kings 17), the contest with the four hundred

---

3. I draw here from my article "What the Biblical Scribes Teach Us," 659.

prophets of Baal (chapter 18), his return to Horeb/Sinai for renewal (chapter 19), his defense of Naboth (chapter 21), and his ascension (2 Kings 2:12). The Gospel selections that accompany the Elijah and Elisha stories are, not surprisingly, the miracle stories of Jesus. Elisha stories in the lectionary are nearly all miracles. On the Twenty-Eighth Sunday in Ordinary Time, year B, Elisha's cure of the Syrian general Naaman accompanies Luke 17:11–19, the cure of the ten lepers with only the Samaritan returning to give thanks. The Thirty-Second Sunday, year B, readings from the lectionary contrast the poor widow of Zarephath in 1 Kings 17:10–16 with Mark 12:38–44, the widow who gives her last coin. On the Tenth Sunday, year C, the second half of 1 Kings 17, verses 17–24, the miraculous restoration of the widow's son, provides a context for Jesus' restoration to life of the son of the widow of Nain (Luke 7:11–17). On the Nineteenth Sunday, year B, the angel's feeding of the exhausted Elisha provides a context for Jesus' Bread of Life discourse in John 6. These are only some of the ways in which Elijah and Elisha speak to believers today.

CHAPTER 3

Prophets in the Bible: The Writing Prophets

Introducing the Third Cluster of Prophetic Books: The Writing Prophets

Chapter 2 surveyed the prophets during the early days of the monarchy in the late eleventh and tenth centuries and looked at the prophets Elijah and Elisha of a century later. By the middle of the eighth century (around 750 BC), prophets had been active in Israel for more than two-and-a-half centuries. In the mid-eighth century, however, something unprecedented took place that changed the face of biblical prophecy forever. Prophets again became active, but this time their words as well as their deeds were remembered and copied on papyrus or leather scrolls that later generations could read (or have read to them).

The first of this new type of writing prophet was a farmer named Amos, who hailed from Tekoa, a small town in the Judean hills south of Bethlehem. Though from the Southern Kingdom of Judah, he was commanded to preach in the Northern Kingdom, Israel. To avoid confusion, it should be said at the outset that "Israel" can refer to Israel united and also refer to the Northern Kingdom exclusively. When ordered not to preach on government property by Amaziah, a royal official in the kingdom of Israel, Amos made clear that he was not like earlier prophets: "I am not a prophet (Hebrew *nābî'*), nor do I belong to a company of prophets. I am a herdsman and a dresser of sycamores, but the Lord took me from following the flock" (Amos 7:14). Though scholars debate the meaning of his denial,

37

Amos most likely meant that he was not a nābî-prophet like Elijah, Elisha, and Ahijah, who were involved directly in politics. The denial may have reassured Amaziah, a government official of the Northern Kingdom, since Amos seemed to be saying that he did not intend to preach about politics as such. Amos' message, in fact, concerned more than the Northern Kingdom's politics, but all Israel, north and south, and foreign nations, too. Amos preached against moral corruption and enjoined that Israel worship properly; he believed that the people did not practice justice toward each other, and that their institutions were rigged in favor of the rich. At their shrines, they did not worship YHWH alone, but relied on other gods as well, violating the first commandment forbidding "other gods beside me" (Deuteronomy 5:7). The shrines invited people to worship that which was false. What is remarkable is that Amos' words have survived even to today. How? It is not clear whether it was Amos himself or his disciples who wrote down his preaching. Alternatively, much later on, scribes in Jerusalem could have written down his words, which had been preserved in oral tradition, and may have added material to Amos' words.

The more interesting and difficult question, however, is *why* the writing prophets and their messages were so carefully recorded at this particular time in Israel's history and not earlier or later. How did these prophets differ from their prophetic predecessors? The incontrovertible fact is that writing prophets emerged rather abruptly in the second half of the eighth century. They appeared in three groupings: First, Amos, Hosea, Isaiah of Jerusalem, and Micah appeared in the period from 750 to 700 BC. A second group appeared in the latter part of the seventh century (Habakkuk, Zephaniah, Jeremiah, Nahum, and Ezekiel). In the sixth century, yet another group appeared on the scene (Obadiah and Isaiah 40–66, Haggai, Zechariah, Malachi, and perhaps Joel and Jonah at the same time). Why did all these prophets (the book of Daniel being the major exception) either work *during the period* from 750 to 500 BC or, coming after that time, comment on events *occurring in that period*?

With our limited knowledge of the historical and cultural world of the mid-eighth to the late-sixth centuries, we have to find answers to our question mainly from hints in the prophetic writings themselves. Scholars have answered the question in various ways. I will present here one way of answering the question. Their writings indicate that these prophets shared a common conviction, right from the first: the national story that everybody took as authoritative no longer seemed to be "true" in the sense of offering a credible basis for living and believing. That national story was articulated at least implicitly in the historical books of the Old Testament and in the Psalms. According to the story, YHWH freed his people from the harsh treatment of the pharaoh and led his people out of Egypt. At Sinai, with Moses mediating, he made a covenant with them so that he would be their God and they would be his people. From Sinai, the Lord brought them to freedom and prosperity in the land of Canaan. The idea can be summarized in a simple phrase: We were servants of the pharaoh in Egypt, and now we are servants of YHWH in Canaan. The people's relationship to God, as "servant," contrasts with their old relationship to the pharaoh, which is better described as "slave," but the Hebrew word, 'ebed, can have both meanings.

One could tell the story in at least two versions. The most common version of the national story is found in the narrative in the Pentateuch and historical books, in which the exodus from Egypt (which included the covenant at Sinai and conquest of Canaan) was the central event. This was the version of many writing prophets, particularly of Amos, Jeremiah, and Isaiah 40–55. There was another version, however, that might not seem to be similar at first hearing, but it dealt with many of the same themes as the exodus-from-Egypt version. This second version centers on the Lord in his mountain dwelling, the site of the holy city Zion, secure from all enemies, and the Davidic king, YHWH's lieutenant, his adopted "son." Through the institution of both the holy city (or temple) and the king, the Lord bestowed blessings and protected the people. The second version does not differ radically from the "exodus version" as some might imagine. In Exodus 15 and other venerable texts, the exodus journey finds its climax in Israel entering the holy dwelling of the Lord in Canaan. The kingship of YHWH is important in this version of the national story.

> You brought them in, you planted them,
>> on the mountain that is your own—
> The place you made the base of your throne, Lord,
>> the sanctuary, Lord, your hands established.
>> May the lord reign forever and ever! (Exodus 15:17–18a)

Isaiah and Micah in the eighth century invoked the second version of the national story.

Both versions of the national story and their variants, we can conjecture, would have left the people, mostly farmers or processors of farm produce, dissatisfied at some point. According to the story, Israelites dwelt in the Lord's land, supposedly confident that their Lord blessed and protected those who worshiped properly and practiced justice. For an agrarian people like Israel, however, for whom the land was so directly essential for their life and well-being, the dissonance between belief and reality was becoming unbearable. According to Israelite tradition, the land belonged to YHWH; that is, he had *dominion* in the sense of absolute ownership and control of property. The Israelite people had the *usufruct*, the right to use YHWH's land. The people worked the fields and tended their herds and flocks, enjoying the yield of crops (mainly grains) and clothing (linen from flax, cotton, and wool from sheep) and food. There were conditions, however. The land was given to families, not to individual members of the family. Individual family members were not able to sell or "alienate" land over which they did not have dominion. According to Leviticus 25:23, "The land shall not be sold irrevocably; for the land is mine, and you are but resident aliens and under my authority. Therefore in every part of the country that you occupy, you must permit the land to be redeemed"—that is, bought back by a member of the family if the land were to pass out of the family.

By the eighth century, however, the national story began to ring hollow for many people. If we are to believe the prophets' consistent criticism, many farmers' hold on their land had disappeared. In plague or drought years, when crop yields were low, famers turned to wealthy neighbors for money or credit toward food and seed for the following year. Sometimes farmers turned over their inherited land to their creditors, thereafter working their own plots as serfs, retaining subsistence levels and turning the rest over to the new owners of the land. This appalling state of affairs brought Israelites (the vast majority of whom were farmers) back to their original condition as serfs to the pharaoh! As we have seen from Samuel's modeling of the prophetic office in 1 Samuel 1–15 (especially chapters 8 and 12), an important prophetic duty was to defend the ancient traditions of fairness and kinship. The land, which belonged to the Lord and was the basis of Israel's economy, was being taken from the people. At the very beginning of the writing prophets, Amos denounced uncaring rich men (3:15): "I will strike the winter house / and the summer house; / The houses of ivory shall lie in ruin, / and their many rooms shall be no more— / oracle of the Lord." Amos 6:1–7 has a similar condemnation. He condemns also their wives who urged their husbands to bring them more luxury goods (4:1–3).

> Hear this word, you cows of Bashan,
>> who live on the mount of Samaria:
> Who oppress the destitute
>> and abuse the needy;
> Who say to your husbands,
>> "Bring us a drink!"
> The Lord GOD has sworn by his holiness:
> Truly days are coming upon you
>> when they shall drag you away with ropes,
>> your children with fishhooks.

The people at that time who assumed that the phrase "The day of the Lord" referred to the intervention of the Lord against Israel's external enemies will be shocked, Amos predicted, when on that day the Lord will attack his own people. "Woe to those who yearn / for the day of the LORD! / What will the day of the LORD mean for you? / It will be darkness, not light! / As if someone fled from a lion / and a bear met him" (Amos 5:18–19).

Prosperity had become restricted to the wealthy and to those who seized the opportunity to profit from their neighbors' misfortune. Domestic injustice, however, was not the only ill endangering their relationship to the Lord. External threats appeared. City states to the north began to plague Israel in the late ninth century. More menacing still was the eighth-century revival and westward expansion of the powerful Assyrian Empire in the east (Iraq today). In previous centuries, Israel had been able to defend its land against the modest-sized Syrian city-states, but Israel could not do the same against mighty Assyria. At that time, Assyria was entering upon one of its periods of aggression against the Levant (the east coast of the Mediterranean Sea). Israel's existence as the Lord's people hung in the balance. They were in danger of reverting to their pre-exodus state—serfdom and subjugation by foreign rulers. This was the servile life they thought they had left behind forever when they departed from Egypt for the promised land. But to the prophets, serfdom and foreign rule had returned, and they could not be silent.

The prophets publicized the danger in detail, because the corruption of the people from idolatrous worship and social injustice had reached a point where it threatened to drive the Lord from the land. They knew that the Lord could not live in a land corrupted by sin. But if the Lord left, the land would be unprotected, and poor people would be at the mercy of the callous wealthy. A vivid reminder of the absolute necessity of the Lord's presence in the land is the theology behind the book of Leviticus. The book of Leviticus is a kind of priests' manual for maintaining the Lord's presence in the land. In Leviticus, the chief means for ensuring YHWH's protective presence was gift exchange. Israel's gifts to the Lord were naturally those of a people in an agrarian economy such as farm animals and produce of the fields. Gifts of farm animals and agricultural produce had two aims—they honored the Lord, the real owner of the land, and the gifts atoned for the people's sins. The priestly sacrificial system articulated in Leviticus regulated the people's giving by classifying the sacrifices (burnt offering, cereal offering, well-being offering, sin offering, and guilt offering) and giving precise directions on how to offer sacrifices in the proper way.

Serious sins, such as murder, adultery, and idolatry, posed a significant danger to the survival of Israel. If unaddressed, the sins, which were imagined almost as a physical stain or miasma (unhealthy smell or atmosphere), accumulated in the Holy of Holies, making it impossible for the all-holy God to remain among the people. As recent scholars like Jacob Milgrom, Baruch Schwartz, and Gary Anderson have shown, the people's serious sins created a stain that adhered to the very throne of God in the temple. The day of atonement in Leviticus 16, or day of purgation of the temple as it is sometimes known, describes the procedure for moving the stain away from the land. The elaborate procedure in Leviticus gives an idea of how dangerous people considered serious sins, and it helps us understand the urgency of the prophetic task. The prophets were acutely conscious of the utter holiness of the Lord. As the prophets saw matters, the people had to turn from their evil ways, for if they did not, YHWH, their protector and source of blessing, would leave them.

Convinced that the all-holy God would not live among an unrepentant people, the very first writing prophet, Amos, announced "The end has come upon my people Israel" (Amos 8:2). The prophets, however, were also confident that the people's repentance would invite the Lord to dwell in the land again. Israel had ceased to be its authentic self as the Lord's people because of their false worship and failure to practice justice toward each other. Amos' proclamation that the end has come did not freeze the future and make the threat unavoidable. His announcement was not an objective report about the future, but conditional upon the people's repentance. The future lay open, awaiting the free decisions of human beings. Israel must respond by conversion, "to turn" in Hebrew, which meant turning away from sin and toward God. Nonetheless, Amos taught that Israel's future lay on the other side of divine judgment.

In a dramatic move (Amos 3:9–11, following LXX rather than MT),[1] Amos invited the people of Assyria and Egypt to see the injustices of Israel and its weakness from the Lord's potential absence: "Gather on the mount of Samaria, and see the great disorders within it, the oppression within its midst. . . . Therefore thus says the Lord God: An enemy shall surround the land, tear down your fortresses, and pillage your strongholds." Though these two enemies of Israel might not attack immediately, Amos warned the people that if the Lord left and the enemy attacked, Israel would be helpless.

Judgment in the Bible

We must delay for a moment to address the meaning of an important biblical word—"judgment." It differs in four important ways from modern understandings of "judgment." First, the Hebrew verb *šāpaṭ*, traditionally but unsatisfactorily translated by English "to judge" is, unlike the English word, not limited to mental activity or legal usage. A more accurate translation is "to rule, govern," because the ruling function is more important than the judicial function. Second, biblical ruling aims to implement divine justice—that is, to establish the justice that God intends the world to have. In many cases, "to judge" in the Bible meant making an unjust situation just. As a result, judgment in the Bible often seems excessively negative in that it corrects or even ends an evil situation. At certain points, Israel's sins forced the Lord to abandon Zion, leaving the people vulnerable to vicious attack from their enemies. Biblical judgment is not a theoretical pronouncement or impartial evaluation of a situation, but often an intervention into an unjust situation. In the Bible, to judge a situation was to rectify it, that is, to bring it back into

---

1. See abbreviations, p. vi.

conformity to the divine will, though the correction can involve force and even violence. Psalm 75:7–8 defines it well (author's translation):

> For judgment comes not from east or from west,
> not from the wilderness or the mountains,
> But from God who judges (*šāpaṭ*, present participle)
> who brings some low and raises others high.

A common English translation of prophetic interventions is the verb "to visit" and the noun "visitation" (Hebrew *pāqad*, Greek *episkeptomai*). In the *Benedictus* in Luke 1:68–78, Zechariah uses the Greek term to frame his praise of God for "intervening."

A fourth difference between the modern and the biblical conception of judgment is that although divine judgment can take place at the end time of history, as for example in Michelangelo's Sistine Chapel painting "The Last Judgment," divine judging or ruling may take place *within* history and employ human means to achieve it. It is not therefore surprising to learn that Isaiah, Jeremiah, and Ezekiel saw the great empires of the day as instruments in YHWH's hands to effect judgment—that is, to rectify an unjust situation. For First Isaiah, the divine instrument was Assyria (Isaiah 10:5), for Jeremiah, Babylon (Jeremiah 20:4; 28:14), and for Second Isaiah, Cyrus of Persia (Isaiah 44:28; 45:1). Though these kings and empires were far from admirable themselves, God employed them to bring about his purposes. In summary, God's judgment or rectification could take place within history, not just at its end, and involve human agency—for example, pagan kings, whether or not the kings were conscious of their role.

These ideas are essential for understanding the writing prophets. The great mid-twentieth-century biblical scholar Gerhard von Rad explained how he understood judgment:

> [The prophets] believed, therefore, that salvation could only come if Yahweh arose to perform new acts upon Israel, an event which they looked on as certain—and they entreated those who were still able to hear not to put their trust in illusory safeguards (Micah 3:11), but to

"look to" what was to come, and to take refuge in Yahweh's saving act, which was near at hand. The prophets were therefore the first men [sic] in Israel to proclaim over and over again and on an ever widening basis that salvation comes in the shadow of judgment.[2]

In von Rad's view, the prophets saw that the obstacles to the people's acceptance of the Lord's rule were so deeply ingrained that only a severe act could remove them.

Though it may be that not every prophet saw the two-hundred-and-fifty-year period in which the writing prophets were active as a unified process, it seems clear that the scribes who later edited and copied the prophetic scrolls did operate with such an assumption. In their view, during the period 750–500 BC, Israel underwent a process in which divine judgment of the type described above took place. The judgment would not proceed, however, without the participation of human beings. Announcing that the "end has come," Amos (8:2) nonetheless presumed an open future that awaited the free decisions of humans. People had the choice of responding and participating in the new divine act. The prophets were there to preach and prepare the people to respond appropriately.

Whether they were fully aware of a process or not, the prophets monitored every phase of the two-hundred-fifty-year period. Some put their emphasis on indicting people for their sins. Amos and Jeremiah are prophets bent on stripping away the people's illusions. Some spent most of their time criticizing false worship (for example, Hosea) whereas others (for example, Isaiah) preached against social injustice and against the people's mindless confidence in the divine promises to protect Zion and uphold the Davidic king. Some prophets seemed to hold out little hope (for example, Amos 5:15) whereas others boldly proclaimed a time of forgiveness (for example, Isaiah 40–55).

It is time for an overview of the prophets. They will be analyzed in chronological order.

---

2. *Old Testament Theology*, trans. D. M. G. Stalker (New York: Harper, 1962) 1.185, von Rad's italics.

The Eighth-Century Writing Prophets: Amos, Hosea, Micah, and Isaiah of Jerusalem

Amos, around 760–750 BC

To review Amos' backstory, he was a farmer who lived in the Judean hills about six miles south of Jerusalem. There Amos raised sheep and tended sycamore trees (*ficus sycomorus*—what we call fig trees) for their fruit. Commissioned during the prosperous reigns of Uzziah in Judah and Jeroboam in Israel, he traveled north to the royally-sponsored shrine at Bethel. There he preached his harsh message of doom upon Israel. Ordered off the shrine and accused of being a *nābî'*, a term that at that time implied involvement in politics, similar to the involvement of Elijah and Elisha, Amos rebutted the charge in the excerpt quoted earlier in the chapter.

In an elliptical sentence, Amos indicted Israel for failing to obey YHWH's ethical demands given at Mount Sinai during their exodus from Egypt: "You alone I have known, / among all the families of the earth; / *therefore* I will punish you / for all your iniquities" (Amos 3:2, my italics). Amos presumes the people understood that YHWH's choice of them, which they freely agreed to in Exodus 19, implied righteous conduct in which care for the poor was paramount. Besides indicting Israel for its social injustice, Amos was uncompromising regarding the people's worship, boldly speaking for God: "I hate, I despise your feasts, / I take no pleasure in your solemnities" (5:21). The day of the Lord, which the people had assumed was a day of victory over their enemies, now means the Lord was attacking Israel! Did Amos offer any hope? Only a slim one: "Then it *may be* that the Lord, the God of hosts, / will have pity on the remnant of Joseph" (5:15, italics mine). Amos gives no indication that he is feeling his way toward a solution of an unprecedented situation. He, and his prophetic successors, show no hesitation. They are decisive: Israel must ready itself for a disruptive judgement that will restore divine justice. Much later, scribes who could see the whole process, appended hopeful statements at the end of the Amos scroll: "On that day I will raise up / the fallen hut of David; / I will wall up its breaches, / raise up its ruins, / and rebuild it as in the days of old" (9:11). The verse seems to be added by later scribes aware that Amos saw only the dim, frightening beginnings of a judgment process that would eventually restore justice to the people.

The lectionary on the Twenty-Sixth Sunday in Ordinary Time, year C, quotes Amos' scathing attacks on the wealthy's self-indulgence and oppression of the poor in 6:1a, 4–7 and pairs it with Luke's story of the callous rich man and poor Lazarus in 16:19–31. The Twenty-Fifth Sunday, year C, pairs Amos 8:4–7, an indictment of the greedy and unfeeling rich, with Luke 16:1–13, the dishonest steward. The Amos passage supplies the passion and outrage missing in Luke's story. In the weekday lectionary, the Thursday of the Thirteenth Week, year 2, pairs Amos 7:10–17, the royal official ordering Amos off the royal shrine, with Matthew 9:1–8, Jesus healing the paralyzed man. The healing bothered some scribes, who said to themselves, "This man is blaspheming" (9:3), which elicited a strong response from Jesus, "Why do you harbor evil thoughts? Which is easier, to say, 'Your sins are forgiven,' or to say, 'Rise and walk'?" (9:4–5). In the Fifteenth Week of year 2, all the first readings are from Amos, paired with selections from Matthew 8–9, among them Amos' hopeful prediction: "I will raise up the fallen hut of David" (Amos 9:11).

Hosea, around 745–725 BC

Hosea is the only native northern prophet. His book begins with symbolic autobiography. The Lord tells him, "Go, get for yourself a woman of prostitution, and children of prostitution, for the land prostitutes itself, turning away from the Lord" (Hosea 1:2). He marries Gomer, who bears him three children, each with a name that symbolizes an aspect of national history: "Jezreel," the valley where the usurper Jehu brought the Omride dynasty to a bloody end (2 Kings 9–10), "Not-Pitied," representing God's abhorrence of Israel, and "Not-My-People," symbolizing God's rejection of his people.

Hosea's troubled relationships to his children and wife parallel the Lord's relationship to Israel. Deriving his knowledge of the Lord's bond to his people from his own complicated and painful family relations, it is not surprising that later, when he is reconciled to his wife, Hosea will stress YHWH's faithfulness to the covenantal bond between God and people. Hosea is remarkable for his emphasis on divine love as well as on God's demands. Unfortunately, we do not know very much about Hosea's family relationships since his marriage is more a vehicle for his theology than for his autobiography.

Pointing to the way Israel is seeking alliances with Assyria and Egypt, instead of trusting in their alliance with YHWH, Hosea compares this behavior to marital infidelity—continuing to draw on his experience of marriage: "Ephraim is like a dove, / silly and senseless; / They call upon Egypt, / they go to Assyria" (7:11). Hosea also provides one of the most moving divine utterances in all of prophetic literature in 11:1–4, 8–9.

> When Israel was a child I loved him, / out of Egypt I called
>   my son.
> The more I called them, / the farther they went from me,
> Sacrificing to the Baals / and burning incense to idols.
> Yet it was I who taught Ephraim to walk, / who took them
>   in my arms;
>   but they did not know that I cared for them.
> I drew them with human cords, / with bands of love;-
> I fostered them like those / who raise an infant to their cheeks; /
>   I bent down to feed them.
> He shall return to the land of Egypt, / Assyria shall be his king,
>   because they have refused to repent. . . .
> How could I give you up, Ephraim, / or deliver you up, Israel?
> How could I treat you as Admah, / or make you like Zeboiim?
> My heart is overwhelmed, / my pity is stirred.
> I will not give vent to my blazing anger, / I will not destroy
>   Ephraim again;
> For I am God and not a man, / the Holy One present among you;
>   I will not come in wrath.

The passage begins with the Lord remembering Israel as a child in Egypt, even at that time straying despite YHWH's loving care. Because Israel will not "turn" to the Lord in repentance, YHWH will "turn" to Israel, in love. The Hebrew idiom for "to repent" is "to turn," that is, turn from the sin and turn to God. As one can infer from this extraordinarily bold poem, Hosea is the most explicit prophet with regard to God's love for Israel.

The book of Hosea has three sections. Chapters 1–3 deal with Hosea's marriage and family; chapters 4–11 contain proclamations of doom on Israel plus a few oracles of salvation that culminate in the magnificent chapter 11; chapters 12–14 allude to patriarchal traditions (chapter 12), reassert judgment (chapter 13), and promise restoration (chapter 14). Each section ends with a characteristic Hosean statement of God's love (3:1; 11:8; 14:4).

The Sunday lectionary has three selections from Hosea: Hosea 2, the re-betrothal of his wife and renaming of his children; 6:3–6, a reference to "resurrection" on the third day (actually an assurance of recovery from sickness in three days, not of resurrection from the dead); which is appropriately matched by Mark 2:18–22 where Jesus defends his disciples for not fasting by asking, "Can the wedding guests fast while the bridegroom is with them?"(2:19). The Tenth Sunday, year A, uses Hosea 6:3–6, in which we hear "for it is love that I desire, not sacrifice," quoted in the accompanying Gospel, Matthew 9:9–12, where Jesus says, "I desire mercy, not sacrifice." Jesus makes the words of YHWH his own. We also hear Hosea in the weekday lectionary, no less than seven times.

Micah, around 742–687 BC

A native of the village of Moresheth (location unknown) and a contemporary of Hosea and Isaiah of Jerusalem, Micah announced the destruction of the capital cities of the northern and Southern Kingdoms, respectively Samaria and Jerusalem. The prophet seems to have in mind the upper class, perhaps the urban upper class ("Hear, you leaders of Jacob," 3:1–3), because their sins are false worship ("carved figures," 1:7), illegal seizure of land ("you covet fields, and seize them," 2:2), and refusal to hear the Word of the Lord ("O you who lead my people astray," 3:5). The prophet mixes threats with promises of a striking nature. For example, he cites Isaiah's vision of Zion as a place of peace-making oracles (4:1–4, compare with Isaiah 2:2–4) and the promise of a Davidic savior coming from Bethlehem from the lowly clan of Ephrathah (5:2–5a, perhaps avoiding the mention of Jerusalem; compare with Matthew 2:6). He also speaks of the rebuilding of the walls of ruined Jerusalem (7:1–13). The most striking oracle of Micah, however, is 6:1–8, which begins with the prophet introducing God's lawsuit (Hebrew *rîb*) against Israel and ends with the prophet guiding the people's response to God's accusations,

> With what shall I come before the Lord, / and bow myself
> before God most high?"
> Shall I come before him with burnt offerings, / with calves
> a year old?
> Will the Lord be pleased with thousands of rams, / with
> myriad streams of oil?
> Shall I give my firstborn for my crime, / the fruit of my body
> for the sin of my soul?
> You have been told, O mortal, what is good, / and what the
> Lord requires of you:
> Only to do justice and to love goodness, / and to walk humbly
> with your God. (6:6–8)

The Sunday lectionary quotes Micah only once, on the Fourth Sunday of Advent, year C: "You, Bethlehem-Ephrathah, / too small to be among the clans of Judah, / from you shall come forth for me / one who is to be ruler in Israel" (5:1–4a). It is paired with Luke 1:39–45, Mary's visit to her cousin Elizabeth. The weekday lectionary quotes Micah five times, especially favoring Micah 7.

Isaiah

Isaiah will be treated separately in chapter 4.

The Seventh-Century Writing Prophets: Habakkuk, Zephaniah, Jeremiah, Nahum, and Ezekiel

Habakkuk, Last Half of the Seventh Century BC

The introductory opening verse, called a superscription, does not name the kings in whose reign the prophet was active, nor does the book contain any of the indictments of the people, "Thus says the LORD." Instead, the prophet engages in a psalm-like dialogue with God, complaining of the cruel attacks of the Chaldeans (Babylonians) on the people (1:2–4, 12–17, and 2:1) and giving God's strong and unapologetic responses: "For now I am rousing the Chaldeans, that bitter and impulsive people" (1:6; also 1:5–11; 2:2–4, and 2:5–17). In 2:1, the prophet ascends the lookout's tower to wait for God's response to his complaints. God's response (2:2–4) will be familiar from its appearance on the Twenty-Seventh Sunday, year C:

> Then the LORD answered me and said:
>> Write down the vision clearly upon the tablets,
>> so that one can read it readily,
>> For the vision still has its time, / presses on to fulfillment,
>>> and will not disappoint;
>> if it delays, wait for it, / it will surely come, it will not be late.
>> The rash one has no integrity; / but the just one, because of his
>>> faith, shall live.

The last line has turned out to be the most famous verse in the book, which St. Paul cites in a slightly altered Greek (Septuagint) version in Romans 1:17 and Galatians 3:11. The verse, "but the righteous live by their faith," was much used in sixteenth-century Reformation debates about justification by faith. In the view of some contemporary scholars, it refers to the reliability of the vision mentioned in 2:2, not to an individual's righteousness before God.

How the venerable psalm or poem in chapter 3 is related to chapter 2, is not altogether clear. Chapter 3 celebrates the Warrior God's march from the south to rescue Israel. In the book, it functions as a divine response to the prophet's anguished questions in chapter 1 seeking the presence of the saving Lord. The psalm assures all that the Lord is certainly powerful enough to save Israel.

The Sunday lectionary quotes Habakkuk only once, 1:2–3, 2:2–4, on the Twenty-Seventh Sunday, year C, as was already mentioned. There it is paired with Luke 17:5–10, Jesus' response to the disciples' request, "Increase our faith." The weekday lectionary matches the same Habakkuk verses with Matthew 17:14–20, Jesus' complaint about the "faithless and perverse generation."

Zephaniah, around 640–609 BC

Zephaniah prophesied during King Josiah's reform efforts, 622–609 BC, which unfortunately for Judah collapsed when Josiah was killed in battle in 609 BC. Zephaniah focuses on Jerusalem, first announcing a "day of the Lord" in which, counter to popular assumptions about the day of the Lord, the city will be severely punished for its idolatrous worship and complacency (1:2—2:3). Yet the Lord will punish the surrounding nations for taunting Israel (2:4–14). Chapter 3 returns to the theme of chastising the corrupt city, but in verses 6–13 the Lord, speaking again in the first person, promises "to remove from your midst the proud braggarts" (3:11) and to establish a humble people who shall rejoice in the Lord's presence, "The Lord, your God, is in your midst" (3:17).

The Fourth Sunday in Ordinary Time, year A, pairs Zephaniah 2:3; 3:12–13, God's promise of a humble remnant in Jerusalem, with Matthew 5:1–12a, the Beatitudes, beginning "Blessed are the poor in spirit" (5:3). December 21 in the weekday lectionary during Advent matches Zephaniah 3:14–18, which promises "daughter Zion" (3:14) that "the King of Israel, the Lord, is in your midst" (3:15) with Luke 1:39–45, in which Elizabeth says to her cousin Mary, "blessed is the fruit of your womb" (1:42). The lectionary's placement of the Lord's promise to daughter Zion with Elizabeth's blessing on the child in Mary's womb is an example of liturgical adaptation. Each text was composed in a different situation with a different purpose, but both address a young woman with a joyful message, and feel compatible.

Jeremiah, 627–582 BC or Later

Jeremiah began his prophetic ministry in 627 BC, under the reform-minded King Josiah (640–609 BC) and ended his days after the destruction of Jerusalem as an exile in Egypt sometime between 582 and 570 BC. Though his ministry began in a period of reform, the preaching that has survived focuses instead on the disintegration of Judah that took place from 609 forward, after King Josiah died and Babylon began its assaults. The book of Jeremiah exists in two versions, a shorter LXX version (now recognized as more original) and the longer and expansionistic MT.[3] The version preserved in MT is the canonical one (accepted as genuine) and it is the version that appears in the *Lectionary for Mass*. It has three main parts: chapters 1–25, poetic oracles of judgment against Judah and Jerusalem, including sermons, reports of prophetic actions, and laments; chapters 26–45, narratives about the prophet with some sermons; and chapters 46–51, oracles concerning foreign nations.

Jeremiah, south portal, church of St. Pierre de Moissac, southwestern France, 1115–1130.

One of the enduring contributions of Jeremiah to biblical theology is his conviction that Israel must undergo a kind of death before it can be given new life by God. It is possible that he once hoped that reforms under King Josiah could remake the people, but after viewing the warlike Babylonians, the vacillating kings who succeeded Josiah, and the intransigent moral failings of his people, he came to the conclusion that destruction was inevitable. Believing, however, in the

---

3. See explanations of these versions on p. vi.

Lord's control of the course of history and his love for Israel, Jeremiah concluded that the divine judgment about to fall on Israel, however horrible, would in fact bring about the rectification of the people. Even in judgment, their Lord was liberating and forming them as in the exodus of old. This "death," accepted with trust, would lead to their "resurrection." Jeremiah himself had undergone great personal suffering (recorded especially in chapters 12–29) and yet had emerged from it a changed man; so also would the people emerge chastened and changed from their sufferings. Judgment was a process that involved more than punishment. If accepted with trust, it could purify and renew individuals and the people.

In his so-called book of consolation (chapters 30–31), Jeremiah speaks of a new covenant. "Covenant" refers not only to the giving of the Torah (law, instruction) at Sinai, but implies the exodus from Egypt and journey to the promised land. Moreover, the book of consolation also draws on the episode of God's forgiveness of the people after their apostasy (Exodus 32–34). Jeremiah was aware that in his own day the people had once again rejected the covenant. Hence, he announced that the people could repent adequately only if God intervened to alter their interior dispositions. In biblical language, God had to give people a new heart. In Hebrew, the heart is the organ of understanding and deciding. Two things are noteworthy about Jeremiah's new covenant. First, it does not *replace the old.* "Old" in this case does not mean worn out, but rather still in force and capable of being deepened and renewed. Second, Jeremiah included all the people, exiled or not, in the new covenant. Similarly, in the New Testament, the new covenant does not do away with the old covenant. The reason that it does not do away with the previous covenant is God's utter faithfulness to all his promises. God does not walk away from past promises. (Compare with Romans 11:29.)

Christian tradition regards the prophet Jeremiah as a type and model of Jesus Christ.

Christian tradition regards the prophet Jeremiah as a type and model of Jesus Christ. Isaiah announced the coming of an ideal Davidic king, and his announcements in Isaiah 7–9 and 11 are quoted in the New Testament. Jeremiah, however, did not have the same confidence in Davidic kings. Jeremiah himself, a man of sorrows who was rescued by God, became for New Testament writers a validation of Jesus, who likewise was a man of sorrows yet upheld by God. Certain details of Jeremiah's life and ministry parallel the life and ministry of Jesus, so that we are not surprised to hear the disciples' answer to Jesus' question, "Who do people say that the Son of Man is?" with "Some say John the Baptist, others Elijah, still others Jeremiah or one of the prophets" (Matthew 16:13b–14).

The Sunday lectionary is fond of Jeremiah, citing him eight times and the weekday lectionary cites him fourteen times. The weekday lectionary quotes the more negative section of the prophet (chapters 1–25) eight times. This negative section of Jeremiah exhibits a prophetic dismantling of Judah's social and symbolic world in order to rid the people of the false hopes they might still be clinging to. Chapters 26–52 are the most hopeful section. The lectionary quotes the more hopeful section six times. The Sunday lectionary cites texts from both negative and positive sections.

In the lectionary, Jeremiah's famous commission, 1:4–5, 1–19, is paired with Luke 4:21–30, the beginning of Jesus' ministry, when Jesus quotes Isaiah 61 and declares "today this Scripture passage is fulfilled in your hearing" (Fourth Sunday in Ordinary Time, year C). The Twenty-Second Sunday, year A, links one of Jeremiah's famous "confessions" (chapters 12–20) to Matthew 16:21–27, Jesus' prediction of his passion and insistence that one "must deny himself, take up his cross, and follow me." Jeremiah's "confessions" are striking admissions of vulnerability while holding steady, uttered perhaps to model for fellow Israelites how to survive in the national trauma taking place before their eyes. A contrast is Jeremiah's hopeful promise of a new covenant (31:31–34). The Fifth Sunday of Lent, year B, matches it with John 12:20–33, Jesus' announcement that he will be lifted up and draw everyone to himself.

Baruch, Early Second or Early First Century BC[4]

Baruch, the secretary of Jeremiah, recorded Jeremiah's preaching (which we see in chapters 32, 36, and 45 of the book of Jeremiah). More than a record keeper, however, he belonged to a prominent Jerusalem family and worked as scribe in the royal palace. Sharing Jeremiah's fate as an exile in Egypt, Baruch is last heard from in that country around 582 BC (Jeremiah 43:5–7). The book of Baruch has four sections: an introduction (1:1–14), a long confession of sin (1:15—3:8), a poem on wisdom (3:9—4:4), and a consoling poem (4:5—5:9), also known as the Letter of Jeremiah.

In the weekday lectionary, on the Saturday of the Twenty-Sixth Week, year 1, Baruch's promise of consolation in Baruch 4 is linked to Luke 10:17–24, Jesus' assertion that Satan has fallen like lightning from the sky, which strengthens the disciples' authority. The sixth reading in the Easter Vigil service is Baruch 3:9–15, 32—4:4. It praises the Lord of wisdom who has rescued Israel.

Nahum

Nahum is probably from the mid-seventh century BC, or just before the fall of Nineveh in 612 BC. To sketch the contents of the book is to give a good sense of Nahum's preaching: his rebuke of Judah for lack of confidence in the Lord's justice (1:2–15; MT 1:2—2:1); the downfall of Nineveh (2:1–13; MT 2:2–14); and a dirge over the downfall of Nineveh and its king (3:1–19). The great Isaiah of Jerusalem, almost a century earlier, announced that the Lord would use Assyria as "the rod of my anger" (Isaiah 10:5)—that is, as an instrument to chastise Israel—but afterward would "punish the king of Assyria's proud heart, and the boastfulness of his haughty eyes" (Isaiah 10:12). Nahum seems to have been the first prophet to announce that the second part of the prediction, the punishment of Assyria, was about

---

4. This is the broad dating for the book's final editing, not the dating for the author of the book.

to be realized. The book has been criticized for its violence and alleged vindictiveness, but it is important to note that Nahum does not indict Assyria because it devastated the Northern Kingdom and treated Judah cruelly (Nahum 2:2 is probably a later gloss[5]), but because of her sins against God—stolen wealth (2:9), enslavement and deception of nations (3:4), and the use of terror as state policy. For Nahum, Assyria's punishment will be carried out by human instruments—presumably by a military assault. (Indeed, it was ultimately carried out by a coalition of Babylonians and Medes.)

The lectionary quotes Nahum only once, 2:1, 3; 3:1–3, 6–7, a vivid description of destruction, which in the Eighteenth Week, Friday, year 2, is paired with Matthew 16:24–28, Jesus' call to disciples to take up their cross and follow him.

Ezekiel, around 597–571 BC

The book of Ezekiel is a unique blend of forceful divine speech (warnings of punishment the Lord delivers to the people through Ezekiel) and its divine implementation (scenes of the destruction about which Ezekiel has warned). Familiar traditions appear in unsettling ways. Ezekiel accuses the leadership and the people, and he does not hesitate to criticize their most sacred symbols such as the temple and Jerusalem. Unusual for a prophetic book, it has a chronological arrangement: two series each of seven dates appear throughout the book, introducing groups of oracles. One series relates to events in the prophet's ministry, and another to the movements of enemy nations.

Ezekiel received his prophetic commission in Babylonia.

As in the books of Isaiah and Jeremiah, there are four major blocks of material: chapters 1–24 deal with Judah and Jerusalem; chapters 25–32 deal with the foreign nations; chapters 33–37 announce restoration; and chapters 38–48 describe the culmination:

---

5. A gloss is an explanation, interpretation, or paraphrase added by a later editor.

a great world battle, in chapters 38 and 39, that ushers in the vision of a new city and a new temple, in chapters 40–48.

A priest, and thus a member of the Jerusalem elite, Ezekiel received his prophetic commission in Babylonia in 593 BC (chapter 1), five years after King Jehoiachin surrendered Jerusalem to the Babylonians in 597 BC, and seven years before the final destruction of the city and temple. A number of Jerusalemites, including Ezekiel, were exiled in 593 BC, and there were at least two other deportations. In exile, Ezekiel was sought out and consulted often—for example, 14:1 and 20:1, 3. In 586 BC, he and the other exiles heard from afar about the destruction of Jerusalem and its temple (Ezekiel 24).

A narrative thread, linked to the Jerusalem temple and intimately connected to the Lord's presence to his people, lends the book coherence. The thread begins with the call of the priest-prophet outside the holy land and temple precincts (chapters 1–7), it explores why the Lord left the temple (chapters 8–11), and it criticizes false leadership (chapters 12–24). Oracles concerning foreign nations (chapters 25–32) provide a bridge to the restoration of Israel, culminating in a new city and house of God (chapters 33–48). Ezekiel has a strong visual and aural sense, describing the chariot throne of God in chapter 1, the gradual withdrawal of the divine presence from the temple in chapters 9–11, the grand battle that defeats Gog of Magog in chapters 38–39, and the new world that appears in chapters 40–48.

Ezekiel's call, in chapter 1, shows the Lord's ability to appear outside the Jerusalem temple, whereas chapters 8–11 illustrate how the temple's corruption led to the Lord abandoning the temple prior to its destruction by the Babylonians. In chapter 18, Ezekiel delivers priestly *tôrāh* (teaching) about whether it is possible to enjoy divine blessing outside the temple system. After news of the fall of Jerusalem reaches Ezekiel's community (24; 33), Ezekiel turns his attention to restoration. These chapters speak of replacing the people's hearts of stone with hearts of flesh (36:26–27), the bringing back to life of Israel's scattered bones (chapter 37), the dramatic defeat of the enemy, Gog of Magog (38–39), the new temple (40–46), the return of the Lord, the fertilizing waters of the temple, and the arrangement of the tribes around the temple.

The Sunday lectionary quotes Ezekiel nine times, one time giving his harsh message (2:2–5) on the Fourteenth Sunday, year B, paired with Mark 6:1–6, the disbelief of Jesus' townspeople. A famous passage in Ezekiel, 18:25–28, is a priestly teaching (*tôrāh*) on assessing the integrity of a person. The Twenty-Sixth Sunday, year A, juxtaposes this passage with Matthew's parable of the two sons (21:25–28), one of whom gives an immediate yes and does not work, and the other, an immediate no, but then changes his mind and works in the father's vineyard. Ezekiel's well-known promise to replace hearts of stone with hearts of flesh is the seventh reading in the Easter Vigil. Another beautiful passage from Ezekiel describes water flowing from the temple and fertilizing the land (47:1–9, 12). It is paired with John 5:1–3a, 5–16, Jesus' healing of the man at the pool at the Sheep Gate, Bethesda, during the Fourth Week of Lent, on Tuesday, years 1 and 2. The weekday lectionary quotes Ezekiel fifteen times.

The Third Assemblage of Prophets: Obadiah, (Isaiah 40–66 in chapter 4), Joel, Haggai, Zechariah, Malachi, and Jonah

Obadiah, Early Postexilic Period

Obadiah is the shortest of the books of the prophets and the only one not in the lectionary. He severely criticizes Edom, a neighboring country east of the Dead Sea, for attacking Judah when it was vulnerable after the Babylonian devastation in the sixth century. Obadiah proclaims that Mount Zion will be restored to its former glory. He draws attention to the reversal of the current states of both countries and the remnant of Israel that shall possess Mount Zion.

Joel, Possibly Fifth Century BC

The short book of Joel is difficult to date and locate in Israel's history. On the basis of its contents, the book divides neatly into two parts,

1:1—2:27 and 2:28—3:21. The first part describes a crisis in largely agricultural terms and warns the people to ready themselves for a coming disaster. The author compares a military attack to a plague of locusts, which in that part of the world was devastating. Such a deadly assault demands repentance, for God was believed to be behind every event (2:12–17). The Lord will always accept genuine repentance and bring healing and abundance of crops.

The second part (2:28—3:21) changes the scene in the direction of apocalyptic imagery (darkening of the sun and the moon turning to blood), which serves as a preamble to a worldwide battle within sight of Jerusalem. The Lord is victorious and fertility returns to the land.

Despite the shortness of the book and its vague situation, Joel appears in the Sunday lectionary once, and three times in the weekday lectionary. The familiar text, Joel 3:1–5 (different numbering in most English Bibles 2:28–29), "I will pour out my spirit upon all flesh" is read at the vigil Mass on Pentecost. Joel 2:12–18, "return to me with your whole heart," is familiar as the first reading on Ash Wednesday, calling us to repentance for the season of Lent.

Haggai, 520 BC

Haggai, consisting of only two chapters, reflects the difficult days of rebuilding the community and its temple, which was destroyed sixty-six years earlier by the Babylonian armies. Now known as the province of Yehud in the Persian Empire, Judah was ruled by Zerubbabel of the Davidic line and by Joshua, the high priest. Haggai's message is simple: build the temple for the Lord so that the ills that afflict the community will disappear and the Lord's splendor will appear. The prophecy ends with a reassurance to Zerubbabel. Haggai 1:1–8 ("Go up into the hill country; / bring timber, and build the house / That I may take pleasure in it, / and receive my glory, says the LORD") appears in the lectionary for Thursday of the Twenty-Fifth Week in Ordinary Time, year 1, paired with Luke 9:7–9, Herod's puzzlement about who Jesus might be. The next day, Friday, we hear Haggai 2:1–9, in which YHWH urges the people to be strong and work, for "my spirit continues in your midst; do not fear!" That passage appears with Luke 9:18–22, in which Jesus asks his disciples who the crowds say that he is. The rationale for the link between Haggai and these Lucan passages is not immediately clear.

Zechariah, a Contemporary of Haggai, Active 520–518 BC

Chapters 1–8 consist of eight visions and diverse oracles, all concerned with building and structuring the nascent community. These chapters are sometimes called First Zechariah to distinguish the section from that which follows (chapters 9–14), sometimes called Second Zechariah. The reports of visions in the earlier chapters develop the same genre found also in Amos, Isaiah, Jeremiah, and Ezekiel, though in Zechariah there is more emphasis on the explanation of the visions by the interpreting angel than in the earlier prophets. Chapters 9–11 and 12–14 lack chronological and historical references that would indicate their historical context. Some Jews, evidently including Jesus and his earliest followers, favored these texts and applied them to themselves and what they represented.

On the Fourteenth Sunday, year A, Zechariah 9:9–10, "your king shall come to you . . . meek, and riding on an ass," is paired with Matthew 11:25–30, about Jesus "meek and humble of heart." On the Twelfth Sunday, year C, Zechariah 12:10–11, 13:1, "they shall look on him whom they have pierced," is paired with Luke 9:18–24, Jesus' prediction of his passion. The weekday readings on the Twenty-Sixth Week, year 1, Monday and Tuesday, are from Zechariah 8, assurances that Jerusalem will be protected. They are aligned with Luke 9:46–56, in which Jesus makes a child a model for the disciples; the scene is set in the context of Jesus' journey to Jerusalem.

Malachi, Fifth Century BC

"Malachi" is probably not the name of a prophet, but a Hebrew noun meaning "my messenger," which occurs in the first verse in the book. The text that follows is likely the third segment of the previous two segments of Zechariah 9–11 and 12:14. The "Malachi segment" was reckoned as a separate book to bring the number of "Minor Prophets" to twelve. The Minor Prophets are sometimes known as "The Twelve," corresponding to the number of Jacob's sons and the tribes in Israel. The dominant genre in Malachi is disputation; two parties engage in a stylized dialogue. There seem to be six such disputations: 1:2–5; 1:6—2:9; 2:10–16; 2:17—3:5; 3:6–12; and 3:13—4:3.

Texts from Malachi appear twice in the Sunday lectionary. Malachi 1:14b–2:2b, 8–10, a criticism of priests, occurs on the Thirty-First Sunday in Ordinary Time, year A, paired with a similar criticism in Matthew 23:1–12. Malachi 3:19–20a appears on the Thirty-Third Sunday, year C. It predicts destruction, and it is paired with Luke's "little apocalypse" in Luke 21:5–19. Malachi appears twice on weekdays: 3:1–4, 23–24, "Lo, I will send you / Elijah the prophet, / Before the day of the Lord comes, / the great and terrible day; / To turn the hearts of the fathers to their children, / and the hearts of the children to their fathers, / Lest I come and strike / the land with doom." The lectionary passage refers to John the Baptist when it appears on December 23 in Advent, matched by Luke 1:57–66, about John the Baptist. Malachi 3:13–20b, "For lo, the day is coming, blazing like an oven," on Thursday of Twenty-Seventh Week, year 1, is matched with Luke 11:5–13, the parable about the man who is awakened at night to provide hospitality. It should be noted that Malachi is the last book of the Old Testament in the Christian Bible; Matthew follows immediately. The near-final verse in Malachi 3:23 (English versions 4:5), "Now I am sending to you Elijah the prophet," is the basis of the belief that there would be a forerunner to the messiah.

Jonah, Possibly Late Sixth Century or the Fifth Century BC

Jonah is a short story, written with a touch of humor, about a man who runs away from his prophetic commission to preach repentance to Israel's bitter eighth-century enemy, the Assyrians. Assyria lay to the east of Israel, so Jonah flees to the west. He books passage on a ship manned, it turns out, by good-hearted pagan sailors. A great storm arises, so great that Jonah, knowing full well that he is the cause of the storm, persuades the reluctant sailors to throw him overboard. The storm immediately ceases, and a great fish swallows him whole. Inside the belly of the fish, Jonah prays a psalm for rescue, and sure enough, the fish vomits him up on the shore. Aware now that he cannot escape the Lord's commission, he journeys to Nineveh, one of the capitals of the Assyrian Empire, and preaches repentance. To his surprise (and disappointment), the king leads his people to repent. As Jonah, unabashedly complaining of God's softness, waits in the heat of the day to see if divine destruction will come, God causes a large plant to spring up beside him for shade, delighting Jonah. But when God makes a worm to destroy the shade plant and expose Jonah to the hot sun, Jonah is incensed. At that point, the Lord speaks (4:10–11):

> You are concerned over the gourd plant which cost you no effort and which you did not grow; it came up in one night and in one night it perished. And should I not be concerned over the great city Nineveh, in which there are more than a hundred and twenty thousand persons who cannot know their right hand from their left, not to mention all the animals.

The lectionary foregrounds the irony in this story of a wayward and small-minded prophet. During the Twenty-Seventh Week of Ordinary Time, year 1, three days, Monday, Tuesday, and Wednesday, pair selections from Jonah with a section from Luke 10:25—11:4, dealing, respectively, with the great commandment to love God and neighbor, the parable of the Good Samaritan (a despised Samaritan crosses national boundaries to help a suffering Jew), and the Lord's prayer, which includes a petition to forgive enemies.

CHAPTER 4

The Complete Prophet: Isaiah

Why Does Isaiah Deserve a Separate Chapter?

We have looked at the lectionary and the place of the Hebrew prophets within it, and at prophecy in its ancient Near Eastern and biblical context, along with the individual prophets (except for Isaiah). Now we examine the book of Isaiah, which demands our close attention because it is the only prophetic book that records both the somber beginning of Israel's judgment process (much of it contained in Isaiah 1–39) and the positive conclusion of the judgment—in which Zion is restored as a fit dwelling for the all-holy Lord. In addition, Isaiah is the most cited Old Testament book in the Sunday lectionary (forty-five times) and the weekday lectionary (thirty-four times). St. Jerome (AD 345–420) was so convinced of Isaiah's role in the New Testament that he asserts in the prologue to his Latin translation of the book, that Isaiah is not so much a prophet as an evangelist. Indeed, Isaiah is one of the three most-cited Old Testament books in the New Testament in the following order of frequency: Psalms, Isaiah, and Deuteronomy. (It should be noted that David was considered a prophet and so the Psalms were regarded as prophetic.) Significantly, the Jewish community at Qumran, which we know about from the Dead Sea Scrolls, favored the same three books, for it entertained similar apocalyptic expectations. Benjamin D. Sommer sums up the privileged place of Isaiah in early Judaism (321 BC to AD 135) and the New Testament period (first century AD):

> Fragments of no fewer than six commentaries (*pesherim*; Aramaic
> *pišrîn*) were found at Qumran. There is an Aramaic Targum
> [paraphrase] of Isaiah. . . . Isaiah is quoted more than any other

prophetic book in both the New Testament and rabbinic literature. In the synagogue liturgy that crystallized in the Middle Ages, more prophetic lectionaries were taken from Isaiah than from any other book.[1]

Isaiah as a Complete Book

Isaiah of Jerusalem prophesied in the late eighth and probably into the early seventh century BC. The sixty-six chapters of the book that bears his name contain preaching, biographical accounts, and third person reports from that period, but only chapters 1–39 (at least the bulk of it) come from his time. Chapters 40–66 were written almost two centuries later—the second half of the sixth and possibly the early fifth century BC. The Jewish and Christian Bibles, however, treat Isaiah as a single book. In the threefold division of the Christian Old Testament (Pentateuch and Historical Books, Wisdom Literature, and Prophets), Isaiah is the first of the Prophets. In the threefold division of the Jewish Scripture, the *Tanakh* (Torah, Former and Latter Prophets, and Writings), Isaiah heads the Latter Prophets in nearly all manuscripts. Modern critical scholarship, however, especially the scholarship influenced by the German commentary of Bernhard Duhm in 1892, commonly divides the book of Isaiah into three parts based on content, style, and historical context—chapters 1–39, 40–55, and 56–66, respectively, "First Isaiah," "Second Isaiah" (or Deutero-Isaiah), and "Third Isaiah" (or Trito-Isaiah). Despite the diverse origins of the material, scholars increasingly recognize that skilled editing has given unity and coherence to the sixty-six chapters.

Skilled editing has given unity and coherence to the sixty-six chapters.

Editing has made Isaiah a unified book mainly because the book's editors evidently assumed that Israel's history from around

---

1. *The Eerdmans Dictionary of Ancient Judaism* (Grand Rapids: Eerdmans, 2010), 775.

750–500 BC was a single process. The book makes no effort, however, to disguise the diverse origins of its sections. It mentions King Ahaz (735–715 BC) and King Hezekiah (715–687/6 BC) in the superscription in 1:1 and again later (Ahaz in chapter 7 and Hezekiah in 36–39). In 44:28 and 45:1, the book frankly acknowledges the presence of another, much later king, Cyrus II of Persia (559–530 BC). In the historical period during which the first part of the book of Isaiah was written, Assyria is the major empire, in the period related to the second part, Babylon, and in the period of the third part, Persia. Yet the book does not mention some of the major historical events of these periods. Remarkably, the book has little or nothing to say about the seventh- and sixth-century Babylonian Empire that harassed and then destroyed Jerusalem in 586 BC. Perhaps the book's editors felt it was enough to portray only one evil empire, which could stand for both. Assyria, the destroyer of the Northern Kingdom, and Babylon, the destroyer of the Southern Kingdom, seem to coalesce in some parts of the book—for example, in Isaiah 13 and 14:3–23.

We will treat separately the three sections of Isaiah, chapters 1–39, 40–55, and 56–66, and then examine the book as a whole and its influence in the liturgy.

Chapters 1–39: First Isaiah

Isaiah was commissioned "in the year King Uzziah died" (6:1), either 742 or 733 BC (the chronology is disputed). He was one of a group of prophets preaching in the second half of the eighth century, which included Amos, Hosea, and Micah. What caused these prophets to become active in that particular period? As noted in the previous chapter, one reason was that the national story that defined Israel as YHWH's people had lost credibility. According to that story, the Lord led Israel out of Egypt to Canaan, established his dwelling on Mount Zion, and set up the Davidic dynasty. Many Israelites, however, nearly all of them farmers, had experienced the loss of the land they had been promised. In the course of history, the wealthier farmers took advantage of famines and droughts to add to their own considerable land holdings. When less prosperous drought-stricken farmers could not produce food for their families or provide seeds for next year's crops, wealthy farmers eagerly provided both, it seems, but at a high cost—pledges of a part of next year's crops. The result was that many farmers were reduced to serfdom, losing ownership of their land and the right to use the fruits of their labor as they pleased. Such practices and their consequences caused Isaiah to speak up for the poor and to threaten predators with crop failure:

> Ah! Those who join house to house,
>> who connect field with field,
> Until no space remains, and you alone dwell
>> in the midst of the land!
> In my hearing the Lord of hosts has sworn:
>> Many houses shall be in ruins,
>> houses large and fine, with nobody living there.
> Ten acres of vineyard
>> shall yield but one bath. (Isaiah 5:8–10)

Social injustice was not the only evil. There was also widespread idolatry in which people worshiped other deities alongside YHWH—a syncretistic practice expressly forbidden by the first commandment, "You shall not have other gods beside me" (Exodus 20:3), possibly a reference to images of deities in shrines. That Isaiah had to condemn this contempt for Israel's legal and liturgical traditions shows how many people had abandoned the conviction that they were YHWH's special people. Although their ancestors had proudly pledged their loyalty and obedience to the God who saved them from oppression and had given them the land they lived on, for eighth-century people, the pledge rang hollow. The exodus from Egypt and the people's formation at Sinai no longer had meaning. The people had returned to the state of enslavement by oppressors and were serfs once again. No wonder the prophets thundered!

As the prophets saw things, there was an urgent need for Israel to undergo a divine purification that would bring their lives back in accord with the justice that God demanded of them. The biblical word for such a process of purification is "judgment," which chapter 3 (see pages 44–46) defined as a "rectification"—that is, turning an unjust situation into a just one. In other words, a divine intervention was coming. In the process that he and his fellow prophets announced, Isaiah's task was twofold: to interpret to his contemporaries the significance of events taking place in the nation and to model a response to God. That the prophet had to be a model of this response was essential, because the people were not to be passive spectators in the rectification. They had a role to play, especially in the difficult moments of the rectification. In modern terms, the prophet was called to be both an interpreter of events and a model of how to respond to those events—that is, to be a theologian as well as a pastor.

The national history during Isaiah's life can be briefly summarized. Both Israel and Judah enjoyed prosperity in the middle decades of the eighth century under two long-lived and powerful kings—Jeroboam II in the Northern Kingdom of Israel and Uzziah in the Southern Kingdom of Judah. During their reigns the Assyrian king Tiglath-pileser III (744–727 BC) initiated a policy of territorial expansion to the west. States paid tribute and became incorporated as provinces of the empire. In 738 BC, the Northern Kingdom of Israel became a vassal state and was divided into three Assyrian provinces. The Northern Kingdom had disintegrated politically as kings and pretenders embraced pro- or anti-Assyrian attitudes and fought off rivals. In the south, King Ahaz of Judah (a descendant of King Uzziah) paid tribute to Assyria, becoming a vassal in 733 BC. To Isaiah, the Assyrian king (never named) was an instrument that YHWH was using to purify the people: "Ah, Assyria, the rod of my wrath, / the staff I wield in anger" (Isaiah 10:5). In the prophet's view, the kings of Judah, Ahaz, and Hezekiah, had a specific role in the Assyrian crisis—to trust fully in YHWH's promises regarding Zion and the Davidic king. In this task, according to the book of Isaiah,

Ahaz failed (chapter 7) and Hezekiah succeeded in relying on YHWH alone (chapters 36–38).

Isaiah regarded Israel, despite its small size, as a player in the world of nations. He commented on the interactions of Israel and Assyria. One interaction was the Syro-Ephraimite War (735–732 BC) in which Damascus ("Syro") and Israel ("Ephraimite") tried to coerce King Ahaz of Judah to join them in a coalition against Assyria. Ahaz refused (Isaiah 7) and he became a vassal to Assyria. In a second period of conflict with Assyria in 714–705 BC, King Hezekiah of Judah made several attempts to forge or to join anti-Assyrian alliances (ANET, 286).[2] Isaiah may allude to those rebellions in Isaiah 20:1–6; 18:1—19:15; and 14:28–32. In a third period of conflict in 703–701 BC, Hezekiah allied with other states against King Sennacherib. Sennacherib quelled the rebellion, and Hezekiah sued for peace (22:9–11; 30:1–2; ANET, 287–288). Isaiah criticized reliance on Egypt rather than reliance on the Lord: "Do you trust in Egypt, that broken reed of a staff which pierces the hand of anyone who leans on it? That is what Pharaoh, king of Egypt, is to all who trust in him" (36:6). Isaiah 36–38, borrowed from 2 Kings 18:13–20:19, is another account of Sennacherib's campaign against Jerusalem.

Outline of Chapters 1–39

1. Isaiah 1–12: Announcements of Condemnation and Salvation for Judah and Jerusalem; Promises and Challenges regarding Zion and the Davidic King; Assyria as the Lord's Instrument

2. Isaiah 13–23: Oracles concerning Foreign Nations

3. Isaiah 24–27: Judgment on the Entire World

4. Isaiah 28–33: Judah and Jerusalem in Confrontation with Assyria and Egypt

5. Isaiah 34–35: Salvation for Judah and Doom for Her Enemies

---

2. As explained on page vi, ANET contains texts from societies contemporary with ancient Israel that comment on or corroborate events mentioned in the Old Testament.

6. Isaiah 36–39: Historical Accounts of Isaiah, Hezekiah, and Jerusalem

Chapters 1 and 2 introduce the main themes of the whole book—the corruption of Jerusalem, its judgment or rectification expressed through a (metaphorical) military attack by YHWH (1:21–31), resulting in a purified Zion that becomes the object of the nations' pilgrimage (2:1–4). A similar depiction of Zion's corruption, restoration to its original justice, and pilgrimage of the nations to it will also conclude the book (in chapters 65–66), thus bookending the entire Isaiah scroll. Chapters 2–4 constitute a literary unit within the chapters, beginning and ending with Zion transformed. Chapter 5 begins impressively with the famous Song of the Vineyard (5:1–7), which serves as a fitting introduction to chapters 5–11 with its mix of passages assuring of divine love and announcing punishment. Chapter 5 contains two series of threats that continue in chapters 9 and 10, though in a somewhat confused order that scholars have not fully sorted out. The two series of threats in chapters 5 and 9–10 are interrupted by a block of material, Isaiah 6:1—9:7, which consists of oracles and narratives about the Syro-Ephraimite War, forming the core of chapters 2–12. That core turns the venerable traditions about Zion and the king into an invitation to trust in God's fidelity. Chapters 6–8 resemble chapters 36–39. In both sets of texts, Isaiah invites the Judahite king (Ahaz or Hezekiah) to trust in YHWH's promise to protect Zion and the Davidic king from assaults by enemy kings. Ahaz is unwilling to trust YHWH, and his refusal leads to disaster visited upon city and king. In the later chapters (36–38), Hezekiah trusts, and is rewarded with protection and long life. The kings Ahaz and Hezekiah form bookends to chapters 1–39, examples of diametrically opposite ways of responding to the Assyrian crisis.

As in other prophetic books, Jeremiah 46–51 and Ezekiel 25–32, Isaiah likewise has a section "concerning the nations" (chapters 13–23). The chapters lack historical references that might allow us to situate the oracles more exactly. As in the other books, his oracles denounce the nations' self-sufficiency and arrogance while allowing for the possibility that God will ultimately bless them. A memorable indication of the Lord's openness to the nations is Isaiah 19:24–25: "On that day Israel shall be a third party with Egypt and Assyria, a blessing in the midst of the earth, when the Lord of hosts gives this blessing: 'Blessed be my people Egypt, and the work of my hands Assyria, and my heritage, Israel.'"

Chapters 24–27, "the Isaiah Apocalypse," has long puzzled readers, for it announces the destruction of the entire world, not just one country as in the preceding oracles. No identifiable references permit dating for this section. It carries forward an extended contrast between an unnamed unrighteous city and a righteous city, and it uses undisguised mythological imagery (25:6–8; 26:18; 27:1). The chapters are best viewed as the conclusion to chapters 13–23, generalizing the particular descriptions in the earlier chapters. Chapters 24–27 conclude the oracles against the foreign nations by showing the universal and timeless outreach of YHWH.

Isaiah 28:1—33:24 returns to Ephraim (another name for the Northern Kingdom) and Judah. Chapter 28 was probably directed against the leaders of Ephraim prior to Samaria's fall in 722 BC and then extended to Judah. Chapters 28–31 insist on trust in the ancient assurances regarding Zion and urge rejection of deceptive alliances with Egypt. In these chapters, politics and faith go together. Isaiah 32:1–8 promises an ideal king, and 32:15–20 promises a transformative spirit of righteousness. Chapter 33 concludes the section with a liturgy of repentance and hope.

In a change of style and tone, chapter 34 announces a day of divine vengeance against Judah's enemies, represented by Edom. Edom took advantage of Judah's weakness during the exile. Just as chapter 34 has features resembling those of chapters 56–66, chapter 35 resembles chapters 40–55 with its announcement of the blooming desert as the highway back from exile. Many scholars regard it as the work of Second Isaiah. Chapters 36–39 (apart from Isaiah 38:9–20, the prayer of Hezekiah recovering from illness) are a historical appendix that was likely taken from 2 Kings 18:1—20:19. It describes how King Hezekiah believed in the promises to Zion and thereby saved Zion, in contrast to the wavering Ahaz in chapters 6–8 whose unbelief postponed salvation for the city. Chapter 39, with its reference to Babylon, serves both as a transition to Babylon as the evil empire in chapters 40–55 and, by its depiction of the king's pride, hints at the arrogance that will lead to the Babylonian captivity.

The Message of Isaiah of Jerusalem (First Isaiah)

In 733 or 742 BC, Isaiah had a vision of YHWH in his temple (Isaiah 6). The vision of the Holy One of Israel and the prophet's awareness of the people's sinfulness overwhelmed him. Isaiah immediately knew that the people's survival was at stake. The people had to become holy again by single-hearted worship and just dealings with others in the community. In his vision in the temple, the prophet had heard God's unalterable decree to condemn the people (chapter 6). As he stood before the divine presence, he expressed before God the miserable state of the people. He knew that God would send a severe chastisement upon them with the purpose of conversion and repentance. Repentance by the ordinary means of fasts and sacrifices would not suffice (1:2–20).

Isaiah, mosaic, Church of San Vitale, Ravenna, Italy, 6th century.

In this unprecedented situation, Isaiah's preaching had to be different. He would have to ready the people, not for ordinary repentance, but for a divine visitation bringing total devastation (6:9–11), "Make the heart of this people sluggish, / dull their ears and close their eyes; / lest they see with their eyes, and hear with the ears, / and their hearts understand, / and they turn and be healed" (6:10). Such is the gist of the shocking divine command to make hearts sluggish

(6:10) until the cities are desolate. As a prophet, he had to intercede for his people, "How long, O Lord" (6:11)? He was told only of a long and uncertain suffering, the same awful decision his predecessor Amos had heard: "The end has come upon my people Israel; / I will forgive them no longer" (Amos 8:2c), which means I have ended our relationship; it cannot be reestablished by ordinary repentance.

Though the commission of Isaiah to this task takes place in chapter 6, the main lines of the judgment scenario had already been laid out in the oracle about the purification of Zion in 1:21–26 with its explanatory comments in verses 27–31. According to the oracle, YHWH will attack Zion as a warrior and destroy the city, corrupt as it then was. But the Lord would not fulfill the oracle personally. His agent, the Assyrian king, will carry it out, and later, the Babylonian king. They, as instruments of YHWH, will be the ones who will destroy the city. Then, from the city's ashes, a purified city will emerge. Immediately following Isaiah 1:21–31 is the striking vision of the holy city Zion as the goal of pilgrimage for the nations (2:2–4).

To help the people understand the divine plan and respond to it, Isaiah reinterpreted the authoritative traditions he inherited—the traditions about Zion and David. As they were usually understood, those Zion and David traditions reassured people more than they challenged them, since they affirmed that God would protect Zion and the Davidic king against all enemies. Isaiah altered this triumphalist ideology. Since he believed that the coming judgment would end ultimately in salvation rather than destruction, he taught the people to trust in YHWH's plan no matter where it led. One must trust the Lord in the middle of destruction. He teaches that the instrument of judgment is Assyria, "Ah, Assyria, the rod of my wrath, / the staff I wield in anger" (10:5). The people must therefore see the Assyrian king as the agent of God's judgment. Radical thinking indeed! If Israel refuses to believe in YHWH's "plan," it would be equivalent to political rebellion and idolatry (28:14–22). It should be said that the Lord is not condoning the notorious cruelties of the

Assyrian armies, but only saying that even in the enemies' cruel practices, God can be found.

Isaiah's pastoral strategy flows directly from his political analysis. He exhorts the people to rely solely on YHWH and to find God's purpose in the coming of the Assyrian Empire. And he wants King Ahaz in chapter 7 to accept his strategy of trust and to model confidence in God's protection.

In summary, Isaiah recognized a point of no return in YHWH's relationship with Israel. With a prophet's radical eye, he saw, on the one hand, that the people had failed to live in accord with the laws of the Holy One in their midst and, on the other, that the armies of the superpower Assyria were working their will in the Levant, the eastern Mediterranean shore. He saw a connection between the two facts. Far from wiping out Israel, he believed the Holy One would guide Assyria's conquest to "judge" or rectify Israel.

Isaiah of Jerusalem believed the Holy One would guide Assyria's conquest to "judge" or rectify Israel.

If Israel accepted in faith God's guidance at this difficult time, she would emerge stronger and more righteous than before. The choice would not be easy, however, for it would involve judgment through fire.

When one reads Isaiah today, one encounters the Lord who demands justice of his chosen community and of the entire human race, who guides people by means of sometimes unworthy human instruments, and in the end brings about a more just world. In Isaiah, YHWH remains faithful to the people and ultimately brings about a renewed Israel. Isaiah's poetry is splendid even in translation, marked by memorable imagery and dramatic power (5:1–7; 9:1–7; 14:3–21; 30:12–14, 15–17).

Christians in particular celebrate Isaiah for his focus on the Davidic king who becomes, in the New Testament, a harbinger of Jesus as son of David. It is not surprising that the lectionary's liturgical readings in Advent draw heavily on the book of Isaiah.

The Historical and Social Context of Second Isaiah and Third Isaiah (Chapters 40–66)

In the second half of the sixth century, almost a century and a half after Isaiah of Jerusalem, another prophet picked up the prophetic mantle of Isaiah as the prophet Elisha had picked up the prophetic mantle of Elijah and continued his ministry (2 Kings 2). The prophet, known today as the Second Isaiah, who wrote chapters 40–55, does not disguise the period in which he preaches, for he mentions the Persian king Cyrus II in 45:1 (Cyrus reigned from 559–530 BC). Second Isaiah presumes that his audience knows that Cyrus is the unstoppable conqueror of the Near East, an assumption that would have been possible only after 553 BC, when Cyrus conquered the Medes.

Adopting First Isaiah's teaching that God used pagan kings as instruments, Second Isaiah proclaimed that Cyrus was the instrument in the current phase of the centuries-long judgment, only this time it was for the restoration of the people rather than for their punishment. Compared to the kings of the two empires that preceded him, Cyrus was benign indeed. He allowed the exiles to return to their countries and offered subsidies to rebuild their temples.

Isaiah 56–66, the work of Third Isaiah, was written slightly later than chapters 40–55, for it presupposes that at least some of the exiles have returned and that their main concern was how to rebuild the ruined city and community in such a way as to avoid the divine wrath that had devastated the community. This last section of the book, then, addresses people who live in Jerusalem or who have returned.

The audience for Second Isaiah's writing seems to have two locations. Chapters 40–48 address the exiles, whereas chapters 49–55 seem to assume that the audience resides in Zion.

The author of chapters 40–55 was four generations (in the biblical reckoning of forty years) distant from First Isaiah. Much had happened within Judah and internationally since the end of the eighth century. Assyria had continued to expand under Esarhaddon

(680–669 BC) and during the first part of the reign of Assurbanipal (668–627 BC). After reaching its greatest expansion in 640 BC, the Assyrian Empire came to its end thirty years later. The rapid decline is at least partly attributable to extreme centralization, ruthless policies that fomented rebellion, and the increasing strength of border states such as Babylon and Media. As Assyrian control of its southern territories weakened, a local official, Nabopolassar, took the throne in Babylon and by 616 BC had solidified his power. For some years, the Neo-Babylonian Empire and Egypt contended for control of the Levant, a conflict that is reflected in the book of Jeremiah. Ultimately, Judah became a puppet state of Babylon, but its tendency to rebel led to successive deportations and finally to the destruction of Jerusalem in 586 BC. The city walls of its capital city were breached, its temple destroyed, and with its leadership class dispersed, Judah languished. By the conventional criteria of national identity—land, powerful deity, authoritative traditions—Israel by the middle of the sixth century BC had ceased to exist.

At this very time, the Neo-Babylonian Empire began its decline and a new empire and leader emerged—Cyrus II of Persia. If one could name a single external factor that offered hope to the scattered remnant of Judah, it would be Cyrus. The Persian Empire, though highly centralized like previous empires, respected the diversity of its peoples. Taking account of the different languages and cultures of the nations under it, it allowed for some local political forms.

Chapters 40–55:[3] Second Isaiah

Date and Setting

About the middle of the sixth century BC, a century and a half after the end of Isaiah's ministry and about three decades after the Babylonian Empire had destroyed the sacred city of Jerusalem (Zion) and its temple, imprisoned the Davidic king, and expelled many

---

3. I draw from my commentary on Isaiah 40–55 in *The Jerome Biblical Commentary for the Twenty-First Century*.

citizens, an Israelite whose name and family are unknown came to an important decision. (Given the culture of the period, he was probably a male.) To judge from his preaching in Isaiah 40–55, he was convinced that the divine judgment of Israel, a process begun in the mid-eighth century and interpreted by Isaiah and later by Jeremiah, had purified Israel and taken away its guilt. So strong was his conviction that he felt commissioned to announce that the process had at last attained its aim—forgiveness and restoration (Isaiah 40:1–11).

Several factors may have led this prophet, Second Isaiah, to his conclusion. For one thing, the stunning victories of the Median and (later) Persian king Cyrus over Babylon made a huge impression on him, as one can see from the attention he lavishes on Cyrus in Isaiah 44:24—45:13. Equally important, he saw Cyrus as reversing the cruel policy of the Assyrian and Babylonian Empires. They had deported conquered populations to work on state projects in what may have been a strategy to keep them from rebelling. It struck Second Isaiah, we may assume, that God was doing in reverse the judgment begun under the Assyrian king in the eighth century, when Assyria was the rod of his anger. Now, Cyrus was "the rod of his forgiveness." Second Isaiah must have been happy to see Cyrus allowing exiled peoples to return to their homelands. For the prophet, it was essential for the people's rebirth that they return to YHWH's dwelling on Mount Zion. From Second Isaiah's own words, it seems that he thought of King Cyrus as the Lord's instrument (44:24—45:13) in the same way that his predecessor Isaiah of Jerusalem thought of the Assyrian king (10:5–19), only Cyrus was an instrument of favor, not an instrument of wrath. The prophet may have felt further authorization to speak out about this from First Isaiah's response to his audience's resistance by writing his message down for a later time: "Bind up my testimony, seal the instructions with my disciples. I will trust in the Lord, who is hiding his face from the house of Jacob; yes, I will wait for him" (Isaiah 8:16–17). To be sure, these thoughts are speculative, but they have a basis in the text of the book.

Consequently, when Second Isaiah heard the divine decree, "Comfort, give comfort to my people" (Isaiah 40:1), he eagerly accepted God's commission to announce it to his fellow Israelites. Those Israelites, however, had as much difficulty taking seriously the full implications of this good news as their ancestors had had centuries earlier accepting the threatening phase of the process announced by First Isaiah. Chapters 40–55 record Second Isaiah's laborious efforts to disenthrall fellow Israelites, both from their unwillingness to trust YHWH's plan, and from their awe at Babylon's might and grandeur.

Because of the complexity of the situation and varied responses of his audience, the prophet proposed diverse arguments as he preached to them. Chapters 40–55 reflect his successive strategies of persuasion. In chapters 40–48 he unmasks the Babylonian Empire's polytheism and worship of "idols" and underlines its military weakness in the face of Cyrus' military success. Chapters 49–55 reflect a second stage when at least some people had returned to Jerusalem. These chapters no longer focus on the folly of many gods and image worship; they contain no mock trials and do not mention either Babylon or Cyrus as God's agent. Instead, YHWH consoles and challenges Zion (Jerusalem) to welcome the good news and rise to the challenge of being YHWH's beloved people.

Three of the famous four Servant Songs occur in these chapters (49:1–6; 50:4–11; 52:13—53:12), which suggests that the prophet (presumably the servant) is exercising his dual role as a member of servant Israel (the people) *and* as a servant-prophet, modeling what Israel is called to do. Moses played a similar role in Exodus 32–34 when he was obedient and able to stand apart from the people in their rebellion. The Servant Songs illustrate what it means to be a true servant, faithfully serving the Lord and modeling to others what God wants in a particular moment. The Songs remind us of Jeremiah's confessions (Jeremiah 12–20), which teach others in the community how to remain faithful in difficult times. They portray Jeremiah and the Isaian servant as anguished and disappointed

(Jeremiah 12–20) that their own people did not grasp the divine purpose of their exile. (Compare the three Isaiah servant songs with Jeremiah 24, 25, and 29.) Remarkably, the experience of the Isaian servant begins to spread to others in the community. Isaiah 54:17, "This is the lot of the servants [plural] of the Lord, / their vindication from me—oracle of the Lord," expresses for the first time a sentiment that will grow stronger in later chapters (56:6; 65:8–9, 13–15): the individual servant stands for a larger group ("servants") who begin to regard themselves as a separate group within the community.

Theology

The prophet Second Isaiah had a practical goal—to persuade exiled Israel to journey back to Zion. The people's return, however, was in his view not merely a political opportunity. It was a requirement arising from their vocation as a nation. In his dramatic outlook, the people had ceased to be Israel, removed as they were from YHWH's land and dwelling, scattered all over the Babylonian Empire. To become Israel in the full sense, they must do now what Israel had done in the past to become a people: follow the Lord's command to take part in an exodus from the land of bondage to the land of promise. In their current position in Babylon (and other places of exile), Israel was like the Hebrews of old in Egypt. But now they were summoned to pass through the desert as their ancestors had passed through the Reed Sea; their goal was Zion, as Canaan had been the goal of their ancestors; and the servant who would lead them had a Moses-like task. Israel in exile must *act*, and that act would advertise to the nations that YHWH, the God of Israel, was the only God and the Lord of all the nations. As was common in Hebrew poetry, scribes depicted the new exodus with mythic as well as historical traits, as in Exodus 15, and Psalms 77:11–20 and 114. Mythic coloring enlarged earthly events and charged them with

In Second Isaiah, exiled Israel must take part in an exodus from the land of bondage to the land of promise.

cosmic significance. Isaian examples of such mythicizing are 43:16–21 and 51:9–11.

Second Isaiah did not have a "theology" separate from the pastoral project he was intent on persuading the people to carry out. We have to infer his theological perspective from his vision of how the people could become Israel again at that point in their history. In his dramatic perspective, Israel had ceased to exercise its vocation as YHWH's people. It no longer witnessed to the sole divinity of YHWH because its defeat and dispersal seemed to demonstrate that Israel and its God YHWH had been crushed by the Babylonian Empire and its deities. A concise way of presenting the prophet's theological thought is to list five of his fundamental contrasts or "polarities" in chapters 40–55: (1) former and latter things, (2) Babylon and Zion, (3) YHWH and the gods, (4) Israel and the nations, (5) the people as servants of YHWH and the prophet as servant of YHWH.

In the first polarity (see 41:22; 42:9; 43:9, 18; 46:9; 48:3), the "former things" are events predicted in the past and now coming true. YHWH's predictions, unlike those of the other deities, are not simply examples of accurate foretelling. Rather, YHWH's predictions come true because he caused them. Such predictions prove divine power.

The second polarity contrasts Zion and Babylon, personified as consorts of the male gods of the cities and as mothers of the cities' citizens. The rebuilding of Zion (45:14–25) contrasts with the collapse of Babylon (chapter 47).

The third and fourth polarities—YHWH and the gods, Israel and the nations—are conjoined. As YHWH is supreme in the heavens, so Israel, YHWH's people, is (theoretically) supreme among the nations of the earth. Normally in the ancient Near East, gods were represented by images. This practice is the basis for Second Isaiah's ridicule of divine images and their makers (see Isaiah 44:9–20; 46:5–7; Jeremiah 10:1–16): wood and stone images represent these pseudo-gods all too well, for the gods are as motionless as their images; they have to be manufactured and carried about by human beings. Israel, on the other hand, is the living image of YHWH. Israel's return from its apparent disappearance proclaims to the nations that YHWH did not suffer defeat, but only withdrew temporarily because of Israel's sin (54:7). The unexpected resurgence of this tiny nation and the downfall of the vast Babylonian Empire makes abundantly clear that YHWH is God, able to defeat an empire and bring back a small nation.

The fifth polarity, YHWH's servant as the people and as the prophet, requires explanation. The word *servant* occurs twenty-one times in chapters 40–55, in all but eight instances clearly referring to the people Israel. Several occurrences of the term, however, seem to refer to an individual rather than a group. In the early days of modern critical scholarship, many scholars singled out four such passages referring to an individual: 42:1–9; 49:1–7; 50:4–11; 52:13—53:12. The nineteenth and twentieth centuries saw many suggestions regarding the identity of this individual. Today most scholars rightly regard the servant as the prophet or his circle. This book accepts that the prophet is the individual prophet, but it adds the important qualification that the prophet as servant has a dialectical relationship with (is both alike and different from) the people, in that he is a member of the people, yet like Moses and the prophets of old he embodies in himself what the people are called to be.

The New Testament Interpretation of Isaiah 40–55 and the Chapters' Meaning for Christians Today

The writers of the New Testament were heavily influenced by Jewish apocalypticism in their interpretation of Isaiah 40–55. Apocalypticism was a belief current in some circles in early Judaism that God has revealed the imminent end of the ongoing struggle between good and evil in history, and therefore believers live with an expectation of the future, a characteristic of apocalyptic literature.[4] Examples of Jewish apocalyptic groups are the Dead Sea Scrolls community at Qumran, and especially Jesus and his early followers. Influenced by

---

4. This is a widely used definition of apocalypticism that was developed in a series of meetings of the Society of Biblical Literature.

apocalypticism, some Jews interpreted Second Isaiah's invitation to a new exodus as applicable to themselves, especially, for example, Isaiah 40:3, "In the wilderness prepare the way of the Lord! / Make straight in the wasteland a highway for our God!" Just how seriously they took the imperative verbs "prepare" and "straighten" in Isaiah 40 is illustrated in an excerpt from the Community Rule of the Qumran covenanters.

> And when these [the candidates] have a community in Israel in compliance with these arrangements they are to be segregated from within the dwelling of the men of sin to walk to the desert in order to open there His path. As it is written (Isaiah 40:3): "In the desert, prepare the way of the Lord, straighten in the steppe a roadway for our God." This is the study of the law which he commanded through the hand of Moses, in order to act in compliance with all that has been revealed from age to age, and according to what the prophets have revealed through his holy spirit.[5]

The Qumran community, living at the edge of the wilderness where the new exodus will begin on Israel's soil, listens to the words of Moses just as in Deuteronomy and waits to take part in the exodus that will renew Israel. Though the Qumran covenant community seems not to have directly influenced Jesus and his earliest followers, it helps us understand Jesus' own enactment of the exodus. Jesus performed a new and final exodus aimed at refounding Israel. He chose twelve apostles (Luke 6:13) in imitation of the twelve sons of Jacob and the twelve tribes, fed people in the wilderness (recorded by all four Gospels), interpreted and revised the Torah on his own authority, and sealed with his blood the new covenant at a meal.

To explain these events, his early followers turned to the Scriptures, especially to Isaiah, whom they cited more than any other prophet. The first Gospel, Mark, opens by blending three texts, Malachi 3:1; Exodus 23:20; and Isaiah 40:3, attributing them all to

---

5. 1QS 8:12–16 in Florentino García Martínez and Eibert J. C. Tigchelaar, *The Dead Sea Scrolls Study Edition* (Leiden: Brill, 1997) 1.89–90.

Isaiah, because in Mark's view Isaiah spoke directly about Jesus. All four Gospels begin by quoting Isaiah 40:3, "In the wilderness prepare the way of the Lord" (Matthew 3:3; Mark 1:13; Luke 2:27; John 1:23), to assert that a new exodus was underway. The seven letters of Paul contain about thirty-one allusions to Isaiah 40–55. Though interpreters have traditionally assumed that Paul's interest in Isaiah was primarily concerned with Christ, some have recently argued that Paul's primary interest was the community and therefore related to the same concerns treated by Isaiah 40–55.

Chapters 40–55 taught early Christians that God will redeem Israel (Isaiah 45:23 and Romans 14:11) and his purposes will prevail (Isaiah 40:13 and Romans 11:34; and 1 Corinthians 2:16). Isaiah 40–55 invites all Christians to imagine themselves on a new exodus that ends in God's dwelling, beautifully summarized by Psalm 43:3: "Send your light and your fidelity, / that they may be my guide; / Let them bring me to your holy mountain, / to the place of your dwelling." The prophet teaches the people to trust God's faithful love, to listen to the prophetic word, to cast aside fear, and to see through false gods, as they journey to their ultimate home, Zion, where God dwells.

Outline of Chapters 40–55

40:1–11: Announcement of Salvation

40:12–31: Strength for an Exhausted People

41:1—42:9: Verdict in Favor of Israel in a Mock Trial

42:10—43:8: The Creator Enables the People's Return and Rebukes Them for Their Disbelief

43:9—44:5: Israel Is the Lord's Witness in the Mock Trial

44:6–23: Who Can Be a Truthful Witness of YHWH?

44:24—45:13: YHWH Appoints Cyrus as His Anointed

45:14–25: The Nations Offer Homage, and YHWH Offers Them Salvation

46: YHWH Dethrones the Babylonian Gods

47: YHWH Defeats the Babylonian Empire

Chapters 56–66: Third Isaiah

Isaiah 56–66 addresses the residents of Judah and Jerusalem rather than the exiles in Babylon and elsewhere. It is possible that chapters 56–66 were written by the author of chapters 40–55 in different circumstances, but most scholars think the latter chapters are the work of other prophets. In their view, the mantle of Isaiah of Jerusalem that Second Isaiah wore with such faith and eloquence could fall on others as well. By the time that Second Isaiah began his preaching, Cyrus had triumphed, Babylon having welcomed him in 539 BC.

Exiles were free to return to their homelands. It seems, however, that only a modest number of Judean exiles returned from Babylon and elsewhere. At any rate, to judge from archaeological investigations, the Jewish community in Judah was small and poor. Though we do not have many details about the Jerusalem

---

6. An apostrophe is "an exclamatory passage in a speech or poem addressed to a person [typically dead] or thing (typically personified)," *Oxford English Dictionary*, p. 74.

community and its economy in this period, it appeared to have been struggling with the tough decisions that often split communities into factions.

The prophets Haggai and Zechariah, who can be dated precisely to 520–518 BC, permit a glimpse of some of the problems facing the people. One problem centered on the temple. Who would build it and how? Who would have authority over the new community? We know there was much scrutinizing of genealogies to determine what families had the say in the reconstruction.

How could they avoid the errors and sins that had brought on the catastrophe? Isaiah 56–66 shows a community divided and struggling to come up with answers. Importantly, Third Isaiah speaks of two groups, one confident that past traditions would prove a good template for the community as it rebuilt, and the other apparently wanting to rebuild the community in directions proposed by Second Isaiah. Already, Isaiah 54:17 had spoken of a group, evidently following the leadership of the Isaian servant (presumably the prophet) differentiating itself from the main group, "This is the lot of the *servants* [plural] of the Lord, / their vindication from me—oracle of the Lord." Several chapters (57, 58, and 65) depict YHWH judging two groups of people, upholding one and putting down the other. The basic concern of Third Isaiah, then, was building a city and forming a community.

How could the community avoid the errors and sins that had brought on the catastrophe?

The speeches in chapters 56–66 have been edited into a coherent whole; its overall structure is more discernible than in chapters 40–55. Chapters 60–62, concerning the glorification of Zion, is the centerpiece of the collection, for five literary units precede (56:1–8; 56:9—57:13; 57:14–21; 58; 59) and five follow (63:1–6; 63:7—64:12; 65; 66:1–16; 66:17–24). The centerpiece (chapters 60–62) is framed on one side by a lament (59:1–19) plus a brief description of the coming of

YHWH to Zion (59:20–21) and, on the other side, by a brief notice of the coming of YHWH to Zion (63:1–6) plus a lament (63:7—64:12).

Outline of Chapters 56–66

56:1–8: YHWH Will Gather Yet More Worshipers

56:9—57:13: Punishment for the Idolatrous Oppressors
of the Faithful

57:14–21: God Will Lead the Humble Faithful

58: The Fast That YHWH Wants

59:1–19: Those Who Repent in Zion Will Be Saved

59:20–21: Coming to Zion

60: Zion's Glory

61: The Prophet Is Sent to the Poor

62: Prayer for the City's Restoration

63:1–6: Coming to Zion

63:7—64:11: Communal Lament

65: God Upholds the Righteous: They Shall Inherit the Land

66:1–16: Judgment in Jerusalem in Favor of the Righteous

66:17–24: Jerusalem as the Goal of the Nations' Pilgrimage

With regard to the ancestral traditions he employs, Third Isaiah shows the same freedom as Second Isaiah. He does not develop the traditions about the Davidic king installed on the Lord's holy mountain Zion that were so beloved by First Isaiah, and the exodus journey tradition favored by Second Isaiah appears only once or twice. Third Isaiah does, however, develop one aspect of the exodus tradition— Mount Zion as YHWH's dwelling and the goal of the exodus journey (in Isaiah 56:7–8 and especially in chapters 60–62). The holy mountain was traditionally the home of the deity, even among Israel's neighbors. In the Bible, it is the Lord's impregnable dwelling, the site of his victories over enemies (Psalm 48), and the place of divine judgment. In Third Isaiah, YHWH judges between the righteous and the unrighteous (in Isaiah 65:1–6; 65; and 66:1–16).

How does Third Isaiah continue the preaching of his two prophetic predecessors? Like Second Isaiah, the prophet interprets and monitors the same divine plan as First Isaiah. He believes that it continues to operate and that he has been authorized by God to oversee the judgment process as it unfolded in his own day and to help his audience respond to its religious and ethical demands.

Third Isaiah saw that the returnees were uncertain about their claim on the land and about their identity as the Lord's people in a badly battered city. That assessment led him to proclaim that YHWH was rebuilding the community in Zion in such a way that the nations would see the divine glory. Echoing chapters 40–55, he underlined that the nations should see the glory of the Lord in the restored city no less than in the return of the people of Israel to their rightful land. For the Lord's glory to shine on the world from Zion meant that Israel had to practice social justice and engage in proper worship of YHWH, the only God (chapters 57–58). That requirement also meant waiting in faith for the visitation of God that would transform the city (for example, 59:15–21; 65; 66:1–16). The visitation would separate out the true Israel from the counterfeit Israel that had closed itself off from the coming renewal and ridiculed those who waited patiently for YHWH to transform the community.

Third Isaiah declared that living in the city of Zion was not enough; one must live in accord with the commands of the Holy God dwelling therein and wait upon the Lord. This point appears at the very beginning, in chapter 56. To emphasize the holiness expected of the inhabitants in Zion, Third Isaiah invites to "my holy mountain" (56:7) two hitherto excluded categories, eunuchs and foreigners, solely based on their sincere commitment to the covenant (56:1–8). The prophet gives the nations and Israel the same criterion for admittance to Mount Zion: "Observe what is right, do what is just, / for my salvation is about to come, / my justice, about to be revealed" (56:1).

The Final Editing of the Book of Isaiah

As emphasized in this chapter, the entire book of Isaiah is an inter-pretive response to the whole course of events of 750–500 BC. Not only a record of prophecy from the past, it was intended to be a template for interpreting future actions of God. The compilers, however, did not feel authorized to omit or radically alter the traditions they inherited, for they regarded them as venerable and sacred. Editors were, after all, "tradents"—those who transmit tradition—who were obliged to hand on what they received. Hence, editors were often subtle, inserting brief introductions, juxtaposing passages to bring out similarities or differences, suggesting analogies, and placing similar material at the beginning or end of a section to create a book-end structure—to mention only a few of their techniques.

Here are some examples of these editing techniques, which are more recognizable in Hebrew than in English. Clearly, editors linked chapters 1–2 and 65–66 by repeating key words and images: "rebels" and "rebelled" in 1:28 and 66:24; the inextinguishable fire in 1:31b and 66:24; the garden cults in 1:29 and 66:17; the threat to attack sinners in Zion ("I will turn my hand against you," 1:25) and the attack on Zion in 66:6, 15–16; the promises in 1:27 that "Zion shall be saved in the judgment; / her repentant ones in the judgment" (here the NJPS translation is preferable to NABRE, which says "by justice"), and "The voice of the Lord rendering recompense to his enemies" (66:6). The sequence of actions in the two scenes is important. The beginning of the book asserts that YHWH will attack Zion to purify it (1:21–26), which is followed by purified Zion as the goal of the nations' pilgrimage in 2:2—4:6. The same sequence appears at the end of the book, where judgment in the sense of rectification of Zion takes place in chapter 65 by choosing one group over another, followed by the pilgrimage of the nations to Zion in chapter 66. Beginnings and endings of books are especially important, and the similar sequences make clear that the theme of the book of Isaiah is the purification of Zion so that it might shine forth God's glory.

The Theological and Religious Significance of the Book

Early Jewish Interpretation

Isaiah was listed first among the prophets in virtually every canonical listing, and the book's major themes influenced subsequent prophets: that the two hundred and fifty years, 750–500 BC, were a continuing process of judgment, that the great empires were somehow YHWH's instruments, and that the goal of the judgment was a restored Zion and renewed people. Isaiah's interpretation was not unique among the prophets.

Jeremiah 4–10 sees the enemy from the north, Babylon, as a chastising agent that will itself be chastised (Jeremiah 25:9–12; also chapters 50–51), and Ezekiel dares to envision a worldwide battle in which YHWH gathers the nations to defeat them once and for all and build a city from which peace will radiate (chapters 38–48). Though other prophetic books do not address the entire two-and-a-half-century process, they were edited in the light of the complete process. Hosea 14 presupposes the completion of the judgment, as do Amos 9:11–15 and Micah 7:8–20. Isaiah's theology of history influenced the book of Daniel in the second century BC. In Daniel 2 and 7, YHWH oversees the succession of empires and, after the fourth one, introduces a radically different empire, the empire or kingdom of God, which is represented on earth by Israel. Isaiah 52–53 shaped the identity of Jewish loyalists (in Hebrew *maskilim*; NABRE translates the word as "those with insight") almost four centuries later in their resistance to Hellenistic imperialism. The group described themselves by the term *maśkîlîm*, which echoes the same root (*yaśkîl*) that occurs in Isaiah 52:13, and they gave their lives to save "the many," like the servant in Isaiah 53:11–12. Another second-century-BC book, Sirach, remembers Isaiah as a supporter of Zion and the king (Sirach 48:20, 22).

As already noted, at the first-century-BC site at Qumran, the home base of the Dead Sea Scroll community, fragments of twenty-one manuscripts of Isaiah have been discovered, more than any biblical book except Psalms. Two Isaiah manuscripts are nearly complete. Qumran preserves several continuous commentaries on biblical books (the first known antecedents of the modern running commentary) and six are on Isaiah—again more than on any other book. Qumran commentators presumed two things that likewise characterize New Testament interpreters: biblical writers had in mind the latter days, not their own time, and the commentators believed they were living in the last days. An example is the Community Rule, cited earlier, that understood Isaiah 40:3, "In the desert prepare the way of the Lord," to be immediately relevant to them. Rejecting the religious and governmental leadership of their time, the Qumran covenanters waited at the edge of the wilderness for God to intervene so they could enter and repossess the land. Waiting in the wilderness, they studied the law given through Moses in the same way that Israel of old did before they invaded Canaan.

Early Christian Interpretation

NEW TESTAMENT

Assumptions similar to those of the Qumran community influenced New Testament authors. They quote Isaiah more than any other prophet. Examples: the Emmanuel prophecy (Isaiah 7:14) in Matthew 1:23; Israel's unbelief and the idea of the remnant (Isaiah 1:9; 6:9; 59:7–8) in Matthew 13:14–15; Romans 3:15; 9:29; the prince of peace (Isaiah 9:1–7) in Matthew 4:14–16; the servant (Isaiah 42:1–4) in Matthew 12:17–12 and the suffering servant (Isaiah 53) in Acts 8:27–35.

What about the so-called messianic passages in Isaiah, which figured prominently in the New Testament and early Christian writers, though much less so in early Judaism? Isaiah of Jerusalem is remembered for the passages predicting an ideal king of the Davidic line who would free his people from their enemies and usher in a time of prosperity. The Old Testament itself, however, uses "messiah" only for officials anointed with oil for the office they will exercise currently—priests (for example, Exodus 40:15) and especially Davidic kings (as in 1 Samuel 9:10). Though it was understood that there would always be a son of David on the throne, the Old Testament does not use "messiah" for kings of the far future. It does, however, speak of an idyllic future in which the king plays an important role—for example, in Jeremiah 33:14–18. Strictly speaking, the word *messiah* refers to a future savior only once, in the second-century-BC text of Daniel 9:25. In early Judaism, the word *messiah* developed a future meaning, and many Jews awaited a king of David's line to come and free them from the enemies who occupied their land.

Some Christians apply the term *messianic* to any Old Testament passage that speaks of a future son of David. In this broad sense, several passages in Isaiah are "messianic," especially those occurring in Isaiah 7–9 and 11. These texts have played an important role in Christian reflection on Jesus. Isaiah 7:1–17 is the most famous passage about the promised Davidic king in the Old Testament. Around 734 BC, King Pekah of the Northern Kingdom (Israel) and King Rezin of the Aramean city-state of Damascus tried to coerce Ahaz, king of Judah, to join their coalition against Assyria. Isaiah opposed the move, urging Ahaz to trust in YHWH's promise of protection made long ago to David. Ahaz should not fear "these two stumps of smoldering brands" (Isaiah 7:4). When Ahaz with false piety refused to ask God for a sign confirming the promise, Isaiah gave him a sign: "Therefore the Lord himself will give you a sign; the young woman, pregnant and about to bear a son, shall name him Emmanuel" (7:14). Most probably, the pregnant "young woman" was the wife of King Ahaz, whose son Hezekiah will live up to the promise of the name Emmanuel ("God with us")

New Testament writers saw the fulfillment of the oracle in the birth of Jesus.

for the protection of Zion and Judah. Hezekiah (king from 715–687/6 BC) turned out to be a faithful believer in the promises regarding the Davidic king and Zion and is so portrayed in chapters 36–38.

A prophetic sign, being divinely inspired, might not necessarily express its full meaning in the period when it was performed. New Testament writers, who were disposed to believe that the prophets spoke to their age, saw the fulfillment of the oracle in the birth of Jesus. Hence the assurance given to Joseph in Matthew 1:23, that Mary's child was conceived of the Holy Spirit, is explained by quoting Isaiah 7:14 in the LXX, "A virgin shall conceive and bear a son."

Isaiah 9:1–7 (8:23—9:6 in some English translations, including NABRE, quoted here) has also been influential in the Christian interpretation of Christ:

> Where once he degraded the land of Zebulun and the land of
> Naphtali, now he has glorified the way of the Sea, the
> land across the Jordan, Galilee of the Nations.
> The people who walked in darkness
> have seen a great light;
> Upon those who lived in a land of gloom,
> a light has shone. . . .
> For a child is born to us, a son is given to us;
> upon his shoulder dominion rests.
> They name him Wonder-Counselor, God-Hero,
> Father-Forever, Prince of Peace.
> His dominion is vast
> and forever peaceful.
> Upon David's throne, and over his kingdom
> which he confirms and sustains
> By judgment and justice,
> both now and forever.
> The zeal of the Lord of hosts will do this!

Like Isaiah 7:14, the oracle arose in a specific circumstance—on the occasion of either the birth or coronation of a Davidic king, possibly Hezekiah. Any new king inspired hope that the ancient promise to David of prosperity and protection (2 Samuel 7) would be realized. In the first verse just cited, "Zebulun," "Naphtali," "the way of the Sea," "the land beyond the Jordan," and "Galilee of the Nations," are traditional names for the areas that Tiglath-pileser III in 733–732 BC made into Assyrian provinces. Isaiah proclaims that light has dawned for the unfortunate Israelites in those provinces because the new Davidic king will throw off the Assyrian yoke and rule as YHWH's agent. Because the promises to David were regarded as valid for all times (2 Samuel 7; Psalm 89:19–37), an oracle uttered in the late eighth century retained its force. In Luke 1:32–33, the angel alludes to this when he tells Mary that her son "will be great, and will be called the Son of the Most High, and the Lord God will give to him the throne of David his father, and he will rule over the house of Jacob forever, and of his kingdom there will be no end."

Another well-known prophecy about the Davidic king is found in 11:1–9:

> But a shoot shall sprout from the stump of Jesse,
>> and from his roots a bud shall blossom.
> The spirit of the Lord shall rest upon him:
>> a spirit of wisdom and of understanding,
> A spirit of counsel and of strength,
>> a spirit of knowledge and of fear of the Lord,
>> and his delight shall be the fear of the Lord.
> Not by appearance shall he judge,
>> nor by hearsay shall he decide,
> But he shall judge the poor with justice,
>> and decide fairly for the land's afflicted.
> He shall strike the ruthless with the rod of his mouth,
>> and with the breath of his lips he shall slay the wicked.
> Justice shall be the band around his waist,
>> and faithfulness a belt upon his hips.
> Then the wolf shall be a guest of the lamb,
>> and the leopard shall lie down with the young goat;
> The calf and the young lion shall browse together,
>> with a little child to guide them.
> The cow and the bear shall graze,
>> together their young shall lie down;
>> the lion shall eat hay like the ox
> The baby shall play by the viper's den,
>> and the child lay his hand on the adder's lair.

They shall not harm or destroy on all my holy mountain;
> for the earth shall be filled with knowledge of the Lord,
> as water covers the sea.

Like the other royal oracles in Isaiah, 11:1–9 originated in a specific situation, probably the birth, installation, or anniversary of the king. Plant metaphors were used for kings in Hebrew as in English "seed royal" and "shoot." Verse 1 refers to the Davidic line. As an agent of divine justice, the king was endowed with power and wisdom (verses 2–3a) and thus freed from judging by human standards (verses 3b–5). His rule ushers in an idyllic age, free of violence, when everyone will be taught by God. As one can readily see from this poem, royal poets employed a "court style" (German *Hofstil*), characterized by elaborate and hyperbolic language, which since we hear this poetry proclaimed in the liturgy, has worked its way into our consciousness and become familiar.

EARLY CHURCH

Isaiah is the hero of an apocryphal work, the Ascension of Isaiah, well known in the early Church. Its first part (chapters 1–5) tells of Isaiah's martyrdom and details how he was sawn in two, and the other part (chapters 6–11) describes the prophet's ascension into heaven and revelations granted to him there. The text of the Ascension of Isaiah is no later than AD 350, though it has drawn on earlier material, including Jewish traditions of the martyrdom of Isaiah from the second or first centuries BC. Chapters 3:13–4:22 are generally judged to be a Christian interpolation depicting Isaiah's visions of the Messiah's victory and the second coming of the Lord. In another Christian work, the *Lives of the Prophets* by Pseudo-Epiphanius, Isaiah is killed by Manasseh and buried by the oak of Rogel near Siloam. Allusions to Isaiah's martyrdom appear in other Christian writers: Justin (*Dialogue with Trypho*, 120.5), Tertullian (*On Patience*, 14; *Scorpiace, Antidote to the Gnostics*, 8), and Origen (*On Martyrdom*, 10:18).

The chief patristic commentators on Isaiah were Origen in the third century and St. Basil, St. Cyril of Alexandria, and St. Jerome in the fourth, all of whom took a figurative, metaphorical (rather than literal) approach to the Bible. Jerome went so far, in the preface to his translation of Isaiah, as to consider him more an evangelist than a prophet. Another measure of the esteem in which early Christians held Isaiah comes from St. Ambrose, a Christian bishop and theologian who believed that the Old Testament was written for his present age and advised the recently converted St. Augustine to read Isaiah, not the Gospels, not Paul (Augustine, *Confessions*, 5.13).

LATER JUDAISM

In Judaism, the Bible was read aloud to the synagogue congregation in the manner of "two parts Scripture, one part targum." A targum was a paraphrase of the biblical text in the Aramaic language for congregations that did not understand Hebrew. In practice, such reading involved a back and forth between text and commentary. Many of the extant targums, including those on Isaiah, appear to have been written in the period between AD 200 and 500. The Isaiah Targum has explanatory references on the Torah (for example, 2:5; 9:5; 30:15; 50:10; 63:17), Gehenna (such as, 33:14), and the resurrection of the dead (for example, 26:19; 42:11). Similar to Christian interpretations of Isaiah, the Isaiah Targum contains many explicit messianic references (such as, 9:5; 11:1; 16:1; 42:1; 52:13), though the travails of the suffering servant in Isaiah 52–53 are referred to Israel, not the messiah, which was in line with Jewish interpretation generally.

Rashi (1040–1105) was the most important medieval Jewish commentator, influencing both Jewish scholars such as Ibn Ezra and David Kimchi, and Christian scholars such as Nicolas of Lyra. Rashi employed a literal approach to the interpretation of the text, though he took into consideration rabbinic tradition. Regarding Isaiah 7:14 and 52:13–53:12, he sought, among other things, to refute Christian interpretation. The great Spanish exegete Abraham Ibn Ezra (1089–1164) is noted for his methodological awareness and attention to philology. Presumably, these qualities led him to question whether

Isaiah of Jerusalem was the author of chapters 40–66. In Isaiah scholarship, he is remembered as being the most prominent early interpreter to have raised the question of sole authorship.

Isaiah is often read in the Jewish liturgy. After finishing the Torah on the Sabbath and festivals, the synagogue reader remains on the podium and then reads an additional Scripture from the Prophets. Isaiah is the most important source for those readings.

CHAPTER 5

How Did the Prophets Communicate Their Message, and Why Did They Write?

How Did the Prophets Communicate?

The Hebrew prophets were individuals of a particular time and culture (including language and style), and their audience readily understood them, for they shared the prophets' culture and language. Modern readers need to be aware of that culture in which the prophet was at home and how it differs from our own. Let me mention at the beginning two general aspects of the culture that we can easily overlook. Then we will examine specific forms and genres that the prophets employed.

The first cultural aspect is that communication between people of that time was almost exclusively oral. In the age of the prophets, the literacy rate—the ability of people to read and to write—has been estimated to be Face-to-face conversations were far more important in public and private life than they are today.

less than five percent of the population. In an oral culture, speech and conversations were not supported or "backed up" by written material such as notes, newspapers, and bulletin boards. People could not go back and reread what the prophets said. To be sure, literacy in the ancient world, including Israel, is a complicated issue and much debated, though there is general agreement that the literacy rate was extremely low. In any case, face-to-face conversations were far more important in public and private life than they are today. Two biblical proverbs show in a matter-of-fact way how such conversations were taken for granted: "Iron sharpens iron / and each person sharpens the face of his neighbor" (Proverbs 27:17 LXX, author's translation), in which there is a wordplay on the two meanings of the Hebrew word *pānîm*, "(human) face" and (less common) "edge (of sword)," as in Ezekiel 21:21 and Ecclesiastes 10:10.[1] Another proverb: "As one's face to another, one's heart to another" (Proverbs 27:19 LXX, author's translation), which is to say, *spoken* words reveal inner disposition.

A second difference between public speaking then and now was the fact that ancient public speakers, without resources like newspapers and electronic means of recording, had to make sure the audience in front of them understood them immediately and accurately. To ensure that such communication happened, ancient speakers expressed themselves in "registers" familiar to their hearers. "Register" is a technical term in linguistics for the varieties of language a speaker uses in a particular social context. Good speakers in any period and culture employ language and style familiar to their hearers.

In an oral culture, people had to rely on what they heard or what their neighbor heard.

Especially important was this concern in an oral culture where written records were few and were inaccessible to most people. People had to rely on what they heard or what a neighbor heard.

Register plays an important role for modern speakers too. We instinctively use specific registers of speech when giving a business report, conversing with close friends, or consoling a friend at a serious loss. We are also accustomed to register in reading. We know, for example, what to expect in the sports page of a newspaper in contrast to the editorial page. In reading the sports page, we expect exaggeration, colorful metaphors, slang, partisanship, whereas in the

---

1. The book of Ecclesiastes is known as Quoheleth in the Hebrew Bible.

editorial page we look for careful word choice, a sober style, and a certain balance of viewpoints. We sense the differences between registers because we are natives of the culture that employs them. Ancient literature, on the other hand, requires us to stop at the threshold and inquire further. "The past is a foreign country; they do things differently there," as L. P. Hartley observed in his 1953 novel.[2] This saying is especially true in the case of the prophets, who reflect not only a different time, but also a different culture.

The paragraphs below list some of the prophets' favorite forms and genres that make up the prophets' register. Though *form* and *genre* are often used interchangeably, it is useful for our purposes to define *form* as a specific type of speech used at a particular time and place (more historical) and *genre* as less defined by its original time and place, but rather in a particular way (more rhetorical), and thus fairly common in modern communication. An example of a form is a prophetic commission account, and an example of a genre is an allegory.

Selected Prophetic Forms

1. COMMISSIONING REPORT OF A PROPHET

One of the most important forms of prophetic speech was the report of the prophet's commissioning, for prophets (apart from court prophets) did not have an institutional base and needed credentials from another authority. Amos, for example, declares to the royal official who challenged his authority to speak of the king, "I am not a prophet, nor do I belong to a company of prophets. I am a herdsman and dresser of sycamores, but the Lord took me from following the flock, and the Lord said to me, 'Go, prophesy to my people Israel'" (Amos 7:14–15). Most commissioning reports are lengthy, for example, Isaiah 6; 40:1–11, Jeremiah 1:4–10; and Ezekiel 1:1—3:15.

These commissions contain a dialogue between God or a heavenly being and the prophet. The prophet may bring up objections to accepting the commission, which God responds to by conversation.

---

2. *The Go-Between.*

Sometimes the reluctant prophet is given a sign as a pledge of later divine help.

The sequence of call-objection-dialogue or sign-acceptance was already evident in the call of Moses in Exodus 3–4; it is replicated in the call of Jeremiah, which seems to suggest that Jeremiah was continuing in the footsteps of Moses (compare with Deuteronomy 18:13: "A prophet like me [Moses] will the Lord, your God, raise up for you among your own kindred"). In the two Isaian calls, the prophet finds himself in the midst of the heavenly assembly—no explanation is given how he got there—and he agrees to deliver the divine message, though not without mentioning the suffering and depleted state of the people. The commissioning account functions like the diploma that doctors or professors post in their offices.

God addresses Jeremiah in the opening initial to the book of Jeremiah, Winchester Bible, 1160–75.

2. REPORT OF A VISION

Vision reports appear in the eighth and seventh centuries in Amos 7–9 and Jeremiah 1 and 24, in the sixth century to Zechariah 1–6, and in the second century to Daniel 7–8. One can trace a development in form and content beginning with Amos 7:1–3: "This is what the Lord God showed me: He was forming a locust swarm when the late growth began to come up (the late growth after the king's mowing). When they had finished eating the grass in the land, I said: 'Forgive, O Lord God! / How can Jacob survive? / He is so small!' The Lord relented concerning this. 'This shall not be,' said the Lord God" (author's translation). Note the simplicity of Amos' vision. The prophet himself can translate the vision into words. Jeremiah 1:11–12 is another example of an easily interpreted vison: "The word of the

Lord came to me: What do you see, Jeremiah? 'I see a branch of the almond tree,' I replied. Then the Lord said to me: You have seen well, for I am watching over my word to carry it out." Jeremiah can easily understand the vision, which contains an obvious wordplay on Hebrew *maqqēl šāqēd*, "branch of an almond tree" and *šōqēd*, "I am watching over."

Two and a half centuries later, the genre had become much more complex, as is evident in the vision reports in Zechariah 1–6. The vision report became longer, and, it seems, more remote from the viewer and needing interpretation by a heavenly being.

> The word of the Lord came to the prophet Zechariah, son of Berechiah, son of Iddo. . . . I looked out in the night, and there was a man mounted on a red horse standing in the shadows among myrtle trees; and behind him were red, sorrel, and white horses. I asked, "What are these, my lord?" Then the angel who spoke with me answered, "I will show you what these are." Then the man who was standing among the myrtle trees spoke up and said, "These are the ones whom the Lord has sent to patrol the earth." And they answered the angel of the Lord, who was standing among the myrtle trees: "We have been patrolling the earth, and now the whole earth rests quietly." Then the angel of the Lord replied, "Lord of hosts, how long will you be without mercy for Jerusalem and the cities of Judah that have felt your anger these seventy years?" To the angel who spoke with me, the Lord replied favorably, with comforting words. (Zechariah 1:1, 8–13)

Such reports presume that people in the ancient Near East accepted without question divine causality; they also took for granted that the gods existed and *were active* in human affairs, and that they communicated with human beings, and that some human beings had access to divine plans.

3. Report of a Prophetic Symbolic Act

On a number of occasions, God told the prophet to perform a symbolic action. YHWH commanded that Hosea marry a woman who was a prostitute (Hosea 1), that Jeremiah wear and then bury a linen loincloth (Jeremiah 13), and that Ezekiel build a miniature city of bricks showing a siege (Ezekiel 4:1–3). Such commands were invitations to do "street theatre"; to perform an action that will provoke people to ask questions. A good example is Ezekiel 24:19–22, when Ezekiel is forbidden to mourn the death of his wife, and the people are bewildered.

> Then the people asked me, "Will you not tell us what all these things you are doing mean for us?" I said to them, The word of the Lord came to me: Say to the house of Israel: Thus says the Lord God: I will now desecrate my sanctuary, the pride of your strength, the delight of your eyes, the concern of your soul. The sons and daughters you left behind shall fall by the sword. Then you shall do as I have done, not covering your beards nor eating the bread of mourning.

Such reports of symbols are a reminder that God sometimes communicated with humans by means other than words. A symbol invites questions. God's Word is not simply information, but a word that invites reflection and requires the prophet to communicate it effectively.

4. MESSENGER REPORT

The ancient world had scrolls, not books. Scrolls were expensive to produce and difficult to consult. Readers had to know in advance where in the scroll to look and unroll it carefully for they were fragile and eventually wore out. It has been estimated that scrolls in use lasted about two centuries. People accustomed to electronic means of communication can underestimate the inaccessibility of written material, the near exclusive reliance on oral communication, and the importance of memorization in the ancient world. To safeguard against inaccuracy and deliberate attempts to deceive, messengers were under an obligation to repeat the original words of those who commissioned them.

Messenger-communication left its mark on the prophetic books. One of the most obvious was the omnipresence of the so-called messenger formula—for example, "Thus says King So and So." Judges 11:14–15 is a good example: "Again Jephthah [an Israelite chieftain] sent messengers to the king of the Ammonites, saying to him, 'This is what Jephthah says: Israelites did not take the land of Moab or the land of the Ammonites.'" For similar examples, see Numbers 22:15–16; 1 Kings 2:30; 2 Chronicles 36:23; and Ezra 1:2.

A good example of messenger-communication is the commissioning scene in Isaiah 6:8, "Then I heard the voice of the Lord saying, 'Whom shall I send? Who will go for us?' 'Here I am,' I said; 'send me!'" The prophet then hears the voice of the Lord decreeing destruction of the people and agrees to communicate the grim message. Almost two centuries later, Second Isaiah seems to allude to that original decree of destruction, only this time he hears a decree of forgiveness and restoration in Isaiah 40:1–11. "'Comfort, give comfort to my people'/ . . . A voice says, 'Proclaim!'/ I [the Second Isaiah] answer, 'What shall I proclaim?'/ . . . [a member of the heavenly assembly says to him] Go up onto a high mountain, / Zion, herald of good news!"

In verse 9, the prophet commands Zion, personified as a woman, to announce the decree to the cities and towns of Judah. Imagined literally, the command is strange—a city going up to a high mountain to make an announcement. In this case, however, the city is personified, which was not unusual in ancient Near Eastern literature, including Israel's literature. Isaiah 6 clarifies the meaning of the verse of Second Isaiah. In Isaiah 6:11, God announced that destruction would continue upon Israel, "Until the cities are desolate, / without inhabitants, / Houses without people, / and the land is a desolate waste." In 40:9, Zion, the once-desolate city, will herself stand up and proclaim to the ruined cities and towns that the Lord will arrive like a shepherd leading his flock (40:10–11).

In diplomatic communication of the period, kings customarily sent two messengers (as a check on each other's accuracy), entrusting them with a message to memorize and, on arrival, to recite the message using the introductory formula, "Thus says King X." The Hebrew verb meaning "to send" is the ordinary verb for commissioning a messenger, and the verb in messages sometimes seems to be synonymous with the verb meaning "employ." Prophets often use the messenger formula, "Thus says the Lord," to introduce their oracles.

From the frequency of the messenger formula in the prophetic books, we should not, however, conclude that the prophets were merely messengers. They express their ministry in a myriad of ways, demonstrating they are not simply repeating literally a particular vision or a particular message. They pondered what they saw and heard and elaborated it in their own way.

5. COVENANT LAWSUIT (HEBREW RÎB)

Israel became a people at Sinai, having experienced YHWH's liberation and formation. In the course of time, Israel strayed from its vocation to be the Lord's own people. The prophets were keenly aware of the ethical obligations of the covenant, which is concisely summarized by Amos, in 3:1–2:

> Hear this word, Israelites, that the Lord speaks
> concerning you,
> concerning the whole family I brought up from the land
> of Egypt:
> You alone I have known,
> among all the families of the earth;
> Therefore I will punish you
> for all your iniquities.

Several prophets announced that the Lord had initiated a lawsuit (Hebrew *rîb*) against Israel for breach of contract. This seems to be the case Isaiah 1:2–20, which uses covenant language such as calling upon heaven and earth as witnesses of Israel's breach of covenant (Isaiah 1:2). Heaven and earth plus other cosmic pairs and divinities were routinely invoked as witnesses to ancient Near Eastern treaties. Now those witnesses are invoked to tell the truth about violations of the covenant. Similar lawsuits are found in Deuteronomy 32, Micah 6:1–8, and Psalm 50.

6. SAYINGS ABOUT THE DAY OF THE LORD

The "day of the Lord" is the occasion for the prophets to shock the people by recasting a traditional positive divine intervention as a day of disaster for Israel. The "day" was a traditional expression for YHWH's intervention to rescue Israel in distress. Amos 5:18–20 is a good example.

> Woe to those who yearn
>   for the day of the Lord!
> What will the day of the Lord mean for you?
>   It will be darkness, not light!
> As if someone fled from a lion
>   and a bear met him;
> Or as if on entering the house
>   he rested his hand against the wall,
>   and a snake bit it.
> Truly, the day of the Lord will be darkness, not light,
>   gloom without any brightness!

One can compare Isaiah 13:9; Ezekiel 30:3; Zephaniah 1:9–10; and Joel 1:15 for similar sentiments. The form takes a revered and positive symbol and turns it on its head in order to warn people.

A modern example might be to cite an ideal from the American Declaration of Independence of 1776—for example, "all men are created equal"—and remind hearers about the persistence of racism in the United States. The purpose is not to indict, but to help people to convert in a true Gospel sense of turning their hearts and minds to God and their neighbor.

Selected Prophetic Genres

I. DIALOGUE

The prophetic dialogue presents discourse between two parties. Some prophetic commissions have dialogue, one notable example being Jeremiah's commission in Jeremiah 1:4–10, which in turn seems to refer to the dialogic call of Moses in Exodus 3–4. Another example is Jeremiah 14:11–13:

> Then the Lord said to me: Do not intercede for the well-being of this people. If they fast, I will not listen to their supplication. If they sacrifice burnt offerings or grain offerings, I will take no pleasure in

them. Rather, I will destroy them with the sword, famine, and plague. "Ah! Lord God," I replied, "it is the prophets who say to them, 'You shall not see the sword; famine shall not befall you. Indeed, I will give you lasting peace in this place.'"

Not included in the quote above is Jeremiah's further intercession for the people, even though he is thoroughly frustrated by the people's willingness to listen to the lies of false prophets telling them what they want to hear. Such dialogue shows the prophet's occasional puzzlement and even resistance to the divine Word. The prophet is not a mere messenger, but someone who struggles to understand God's word in frequently ambiguous situations.

2. Lament

The lament is a common genre in the Psalms and a chance for the prophet to express his dismay at the impending destruction of the people. Psalm laments express the unjust situation in which the psalmist is caught in order to move the just God to intervene. How can a just God allow the injustice the psalmist must endure? The same goal seems true of the prophetic use of the genre. Jeremiah's famous confessions in chapters 11–20 verify that usage. The first two, Jeremiah 11:18–23 and 12:1–6, use sheep and shepherd imagery to make their point. Having suffered like an innocent lamb, the prophet cries out to God for rescue. The confessions also model to the people how they, like the suffering Jeremiah, can survive their present anguish. If Jeremiah can do it, so can they.

The remarks above on how the prophets wrote their message and how they communicated it to the people shows several things. They show, first, that the prophets had to wrestle with God's Word. Exactly what they saw and heard is not necessarily what they finally communicated. It is very difficult to know for certain what the prophet's original experience was. Did Hosea actually hear the words that we read in Hosea 1–3? Alternatively, did he perhaps only gradually see the parallel between his own family life and the life of his people Israel with YHWH? He was inspired, of course, but had to struggle to make sense of his marriage and family life no less than he had to struggle to make sense of YHWH's relationship to Israel. Once Hosea "got" it, he then had to find the best means of communicating God's message to the people. Like every "public intellectual" he had to find the best means of communicating with the people. The entire process was inspired, but the prophet's own experience and imagination were involved in that inspiration.

3. PRAYER

Though we ordinarily think of prayer as confined to the Psalms, it also occurs in the prophets, though, as one might expect, integrated into the prophets' strategy to arouse and convert the nation. One example of a prayer is Isaiah 12, which concludes chapters 1–11, the first literary unit in the prophet's writing. The prayer begins, "On that day, you will say: / I give you thanks, O Lord; / though you have been angry with me, / your anger has abated, and you have consoled me. / God indeed is my salvation; / I am confident and unafraid. / For the Lord is my strength and my might, / and he has been my salvation" (12:1–2). Isaiah's prayer is a subtle way of saying to people that if you heed the promises and warnings of chapters 1–11, divine anger will be dispelled and God will become your savior.

Another prayer that is an integral part of a prophet's message is Jonah's prayer uttered in the belly of the fish that swallowed him. Jonah prays as if he is already dead in Sheol. God rescues him from death. "Then the Lord commanded the fish to vomit Jonah upon dry land" (2:11). The compassionate God accepts at face value the disobedient prophet's repentance, but the disobedient prophet later is enraged by God being merciful to the repentant people of Nineveh. That Jonah laments in the belly of the fish and that God hears him points to God's greater mercy in accepting the lament of the people of Nineveh.

4. PERSONIFICATION

A memorable example is Hebrew *bat îyôn*, literally "Daughter Zion," and is so translated by NRSV and NABRE. NJPS renders more suitably, "Fair Zion," expressing sensitively the ancient Near Eastern metaphor of the city as bride of its patron god and mother of its inhabitants. The symbolism invests Jeremiah 4:31 with deep emotion:

> Yes, I hear the cry, like that of a woman in labor,
>> like the anguish of a mother bearing her first child—
> The cry of daughter Zion [in NABRE] Fair Zion [in
>> NJPS] gasping,
>> as she stretches out her hands:
> "Ah, woe is me! I sink exhausted
>> before my killers!"

Micah 4:8 offers a positive picture of Fair Zion: "And you, O tower of the flock, / hill of daughter Zion! ["Fair Zion" in NJPS] / To you it shall come: / the former dominion shall be restored, / the reign of daughter Jerusalem [Fair Jerusalem in JNPS]." Isaiah chapters 40–55 refer to Fair Zion often, consoling her who is bereft of husband (YHWH) and children (inhabitants of Jerusalem) with memorable assurances of the return of both in chapter 49. Isaiah 47 predicts that Fair Babylon will suffer the same dire fate as Zion.

Why Did the Prophets Write?

The Prophets' Agenda: Accepting God's Judgment

The prophets preached a coming judgment of the Lord, which can misleadingly lend a negative and denunciatory quality to their preaching. We should recall from chapter 3 (pages 44–46), however, that "judgment" is not necessarily bad or destructive. It is rather an intervention by God to bring a people or a situation into line with divine justice—in biblical terminology, to uphold the righteous and put down the wicked. Hence, the underlying strategy of the prophets was positive—rectification, not destruction. They prepared the people to accept the Lord's corrective measures, harsh as they might be (since they were sometimes carried out by unwitting human agents), and they brought the people to the holiness the Lord desires. The prophets were perceptive about God, profoundly aware of his insistence that his people be faithful, loving, and just. And they were realistic about the people, their fellow Israelites, aware that they tilted toward rebellion and forgetfulness, yet were capable of repentance, of turning away from sin and toward God. The prophets never gave up on the people and kept on preaching and hoping.

It may help us to understand what the prophets wanted the people to do in response to their preaching. In a word, they wanted the people to repent, to turn. To understand this goal of prophecy, it is important to grasp the Old Testament concept of *šûb*, "to turn, to convert," by comparing it with the New Testament concept of conversion. The New Testament concept is generally expressed by the Greek verb *metanoeō*, "to change one's mind; feel remorse, repent, be converted," and the Greek noun *metanoia*, "repentance, turning about, conversion." Both the Hebrew verb and the Greek verb are similar in their stress on orientation to a defining reality—turning to a person and turning away from a contrary person or habit. The New Testament term puts more emphasis on changing one's mind as well as changing one's orientation, perhaps because giving divine honor to Jesus represented a genuine change from the traditional Judaism of Jesus' earliest followers.

The section above has given an explanation of why they *spoke*—to help their fellow Israelites understand what was happening to them "in real time" and to model how the community should respond to God's present governing. Left unaddressed in that answer, however, is why their words

Prophets spoke to help people understand what was happening to them and to model how to respond to God.

were *written down*, preserved and copied on expensive parchment and papyrus. The obvious answer is that people thought their words were instructive not only for the past but for their present and future.

God was always "judging"—that is, ruling his people—and the community was struggling to remain loyal to God and God's commandments in a variety of situations. The scribes who collected and edited the prophetic traditions and the people who read and heard them realized that the prophets' words illuminated their world. The prophets challenged them to care for each other and to "fear"—that is, revere the Lord by their obedience and love. Judaism has tended to view the prophets as explaining and illustrating the Torah (Pentateuch) for everyday life. Christianity often views the prophets as predicting the future coming of Christ and validating his mission and work, especially his death and resurrection. The challenge for Christian interpreters of the prophets, and indeed of the entire Old Testament, is to understand the Hebrew Scriptures on their own terms, not simply as predictive or foreshadowing the New Testament.

The Prophets' Interpretation of God Acting in the Three Exodus Moments

The Prophets' View of God

Giving a definition of the biblical God is not easy, because the Bible prefers portraying God acting on earth, rather than sitting enthroned in heaven, and especially acting in the affairs of Israel. To the prophets and the scribes who edited them, God was best revealed in the nitty gritty of family and tribal life as well as national politics, all of which was then (as now) complicated, ambiguous, and sometimes bloody. Though later theologians chose to write of God in discursive essays, scribes preferred narratives for interpreting the turns of history and God's dealings with human beings. The scribes wrote down what they saw; they showed rather than explained. This is because their faith told them that God was somehow involved in puzzling and even violent happenings. Biblical theology was *historical*—that is, divine activity was discernible in earthly events.

A fruitful approach to understanding the God of the prophets is to look at three moments when God's actions were enormously life changing and formative—"exodus moments."[1] Each moment had its prophetic interpreters to explain what the Lord was doing and help guide people's response. The exodus theme in the Bible occurs in three clusters or moments: (1) the thirteenth-century Exodus as

---

1. I draw from my article, "The Exodus in the Christian Bible: The Case for 'Figural' Reading," *Theological Studies* 63 (2002): 345–361.

recounted in the book of Exodus and in some pre-exilic psalms and prophetic texts[2] (Exodus I); (2) the sixth-century return from exile, interpreted especially by Jeremiah, Ezekiel, and Isaiah 40–55 as a new exodus (Exodus II); and (3) the work of Jesus in the first century BC, interpreted presumably by Jesus himself and by New Testament writers as a new exodus (Exodus III).

Exodus I in the book of Exodus has two aspects that show up in later uses as well—*liberation* of the people from the false lordship of the Egyptian pharaoh (chapters 1–15), and their *formation* into a people under YHWH at Sinai (chapters 16–40). That the exodus is a central theme in the Pentateuch no one seriously doubts. But only in recent years has a broad spectrum of scholars, especially of the New Testament, come to see its major importance and organizing function in the Bible. We mention only a sample of scholars publishing in English who appreciate the exodus theme especially in the New Testament: N. T. Wright, Rikki E. Watts, Joel Marcus, and Richard Hays.

Exodus I

The most complete presentation of Exodus I is the book of Exodus, which views the exodus from Egypt as the major event in a chain of episodes stretching from the creation of the world (in Genesis) to Israel arriving at the edge of Canaan, listening to Moses' words (in Deuteronomy). The story begins in Egypt when the Hebrews' patron and protector, Joseph, died and "a new king, who knew nothing of Joseph, rose to power in Egypt" (Exodus 1:8). The pharaoh attempted to make himself the god of the Hebrews, negating the dual blessing of land and progeny that God gave their ancestors in Genesis, and indeed gave to all human beings (Genesis 1:28, "Be fertile and multiply; fill the earth and subdue it"). The pharaoh prevented the Hebrews from returning to their homeland (Exodus 1:10) and tried to wipe them out by killing their male children (Exodus 1:22). Five

---

2. Texts dating from before the exile to Babylon.

brave, resourceful women, three of them nameless, did what they could to contain the pharaoh's cruel plan (Exodus 1–2). Moses, well qualified as leader in those dark days, failed in his first bid for leadership and had to flee Egypt (Exodus 2:11–15).

Moses returned to Egypt to confront the pharaoh and exercised the task of prophet before the age of prophets. (The first prophet of that kind was Samuel, around 1020 BC) The Pentateuch twice calls him "prophet": "A prophet like me will the Lord, your God, raise up for you from among your own kindred; that is the one to whom you shall listen. This is exactly what you requested of the Lord, your God, at Horeb on the day of the assembly" (Deuteronomy 18:15–16); and "Since then [the death of Moses] no prophet has arisen in Israel like Moses, whom the Lord knew face to face, in all the signs and wonders the Lord sent him to perform in the land of Egypt" (Deuteronomy 34:10–11). Deuteronomy 32, the venerable Song of Moses, which Moses recites to the people, breathes the spirit of several early prophets. A "prophet before prophecy," Moses interpreted God's great work of the exodus and modeled total obedience to God's Word.

In Midian, south of Canaan, Moses was pasturing his flocks in the vicinity of Mount Sinai (sometimes called Horeb) and encountered YHWH, the God of Abraham, Isaac, and Jacob. Moses' own actions—fleeing Egypt and encountering YHWH at Sinai—anticipated the actions of his people, for they too fled the pharaoh's Egypt and encountered YHWH at Sinai. Later prophets similarly anticipated in their own lives what happened later to the people.

When Moses returned to Egypt, he was instrumental in producing the ten "signs and wonders" (the "plagues," in Deuteronomy 7:8—11) that showed YHWH's lordship over the pharaoh and all of Egypt, even taking every firstborn as ultimate homage. Having liberated the Hebrews and led them out of Egypt (Exodus 15), YHWH won their assent to be his people, enabling him to endow them with the traditional elements of peoplehood—a god (and god's house), land, a leader, and legal and narrative traditions (Exodus 16–40). Moses, who mediated the covenant relationship between YHWH and the people, foreshadowed the prophets.

Exodus I Interpreted by the Pre-Exilic Prophets

The exodus is prominent in the pre-exilic prophets Amos, Hosea, Micah, Jeremiah, and Ezekiel, who confront their people with the claims the exodus makes on them. Amos in the eighth century mentions the exodus as the basis for YHWH's claims on the people (2:9–16, 3:1–2, and 9:7), reminding them that they are favored more than all the families of the earth (3:2). The eighth-century prophet Hosea alludes to the Sinai covenant in 6:7 and 8:1; in 1:9, he refers to the covenant formula "I will be your God and you will be my people" (see Exodus 6:7). Hosea refers to Egyptian servitude in 11:1; 12:10 14; 13:4. His statement in 2:16–17 is the earliest in the prophets about a new exodus: "Therefore, I will allure her now; / I will lead her into the wilderness / and speak persuasively to her. / . . . There she will respond as in the days of her youth, / as on the day when she came up from the land of Egypt." To Hosea, the only way Israel can renew itself is to go through the exodus again.

Jeremiah in the late-seventh century marks a turning point in the prophets' interpretation of the exodus. On the one hand, he follows Amos and Hosea in citing the exodus to indict the people, and on the other, he points forward to the exodus as a future event of salvation. There will be a new exodus (31:31–34 and 23:7–8)!

> Jeremiah marks a turning point in the prophets' interpretation of the exodus.

Exodus II in the Exilic and Postexilic Prophets

The most important Exodus II texts are the exilic and postexilic prophets. Jeremiah's book of consolation (chapters 30–31), already mentioned, describe a blessed future. It contains the rich and often cited passage (Jeremiah 31:31–34) that summarizes the exodus as a new covenant between God and Israel:

See, days are coming—oracle of the Lord—when I will make a new covenant with the house of Israel and the house of Judah. It will not be like the covenant I made with their ancestors the day I took them by the hand to lead them out of the land of Egypt. They broke my covenant, though I was their master—oracle of the Lord. But this is the covenant I will make with the house of Israel after those days—oracle of the Lord. I will place my law within them, and write it upon their hearts; I will be their God, and they shall be my people. They will no longer teach their friends and relatives, "Know the Lord!" Everyone, from least to greatest, shall know me—oracle of the lord—for I will forgive their iniquity and no longer remember their sin.

The prophet envisions the blessed future as a renewal of the historic exodus by which Israel originally became the people of YHWH. Jeremiah focuses on only one component of the exodus, the covenant. Troubled throughout his ministry by the malice of the human heart (the organ of decision) and its inability to respond to God, Jeremiah hopes that God will change Israelite hearts and make them receptive to the Torah. New Testament writers will borrow his idea of the new exodus—the new covenant: Matthew 26:28; Mark 14:24; Luke 22:20; 1 Corinthians 11:25; and 2 Corinthians 3:6.
Ezekiel 36:25–27 says much the same thing:

I will sprinkle clean water over you to make you clean; from all your impurities and from all your idols I will cleanse you. I will give you a new heart, and a new spirit I will put within you. I will remove the heart of stone from your flesh and give you a heart of flesh. I will put my spirit within you so that you walk in my statutes, observe my ordinances, and keep them.

Like Jeremiah, Ezekiel singles out one element that stands for the whole exodus. For him it is the testing in the wilderness by which Israel had the opportunity to trust and obey God. Ezekiel 20:35 interprets the exodus as a purifying judgment in the wilderness: "I will lead you to the wilderness of the peoples and enter into judgment with you face to face." The new testing will, he hopes, finally create a responsive people. God will renew the founding event, bringing the people to Zion, not from Egypt this time, but from the nations where they have been scattered.

The great prophet of the new exodus, however, is Second Isaiah. The detailed treatment in chapter 4, pages 77–82, allows us to be brief here and focus only on Isaiah 43:16–21, especially verses 18–19: "Remember not the events of the past, / the things of long ago consider not; / See, I am doing something new! / Now it springs forth, do you not perceive it? In the wilderness I make a way, / in the wasteland, paths" (1QIsaª). The new exodus will be so grand that people will no longer need to mention Exodus I. The new exodus goes from Babylon to Zion rather than from Egypt to Canaan, roads over which YHWH will lead his people and tame the desert (40:3–5), rather than the sea.

In the dramatic scenario used by the exilic prophets, the people had reverted to the situation of the ancestors in Egypt; they were not on holy ground and they were under foreign gods. In spite of the bleak present, the prophets discerned the beginnings of a restoration and interpreted it as a new exodus.

Exodus III

Given that, in early Judaism, groups such as the Qumran covenanters (the Dead Sea Scrolls community) had a lively expectation of a new exodus that would renew Israel (see chapter 4, pages 80–84), we should not be surprised to learn that the earliest followers of Jesus too, all of them Jews, entertained similar expectations. The exodus paradigm explains how Jesus was liberator and builder of a new community.

In recent years, a substantial number of New Testament scholars have come to accept the exodus as an important paradigm for Jesus and his work. What was chiefly lacking in previous scholarship was the failure to recognize the typological explanations employed by New Testament writers in which exodus was both an architype and an episode in the biblical story. The Qumran covenanter group, for example, repaired to the desert because it rejected current religious and governmental leadership. It interpreted its own situation in language derived from the exodus—waiting in the wilderness until the time came for it to take possession of the land. In the meantime, it pondered the Sinai law like Israel of old prior to the conquest of Canaan. They were "preparing the way of the Lord" by waiting in the desert for the second exodus.

John the Baptist preached in the same desert area, and his preaching displayed expectations similar to those in Qumran. Jesus, a one-time disciple of John, shifted attention to the other dimension of the judgment proclaimed by John—the reign of God ushered in by the judgment. The reign of God introduced by divine judgment could be interpreted as a new exodus, as the Qumran Community Rule cited above did. Jesus understood the imminent judgment of God as a re-founding of Israel, as is shown by his conscious enacting of the exodus—choosing twelve disciples, feeding the people in the wilderness, performing miracles of feeding and healing, presiding at a covenant meal, and reinterpreting the law given at Sinai on his own authority ("You have heard that it was said to your ancestors . . . but I say to you . . . "; Matthew 5:21–22).

Exodus III retained the two aspects it had in Exodus I—liberation and formation. The Gospel of Mark, for example, takes place in a demon-filled universe (see Mark 1:32, 34; 3:22; 5:15; 9:38; 16:18) from whose power Jesus liberates his people through healing. In contrast, the Old Testament regards evil as embodied in human beings such as the "wicked" who are omnipresent in the Psalms, or hostile foreign nations in the historical and prophetic books. For Paul and the Pauline school, liberation consists in dethroning powers thought to be ruling the world, the "angels [and] principalities" in Romans 8:38; Ephesians 3:10; 6:12; and Colossians 2:15.

The New Testament also accepts the Old Testament descriptions of the thirteenth-century and sixth-century exile and restoration as a new exodus. Luke and Paul seem to have developed their understanding of covenant (Luke 22:20; 1 Corinthians 11:25) from the new covenant of Jeremiah 31:31 rather than directly from Exodus

19–24. Luke and Paul view the exodus not only as a movement from Egypt to Canaan but also from Babylon to Zion. In their eyes, Jesus brought the journey to its proper conclusion.

It is easy to miss the importance of the exodus in the New Testament because the references to it are subtle. As noted in chapter 4, Mark 1:2–3 credits verses from three different books, Exodus 23:23, Malachi 3:1, and Isaiah 40:3 to "Isaiah the prophet": "Behold I am sending my messenger ahead of you; / he will prepare your way. / A voice of one crying out in the desert: / 'Prepare the way of the Lord, / make straight his paths." At the very beginning of his Gospel, Mark interprets Isaiah 40:1–5 according to the Jewish exegesis of his time as referring to the return of the exiles at the end of days, accompanied by spiritual renewal and renewal of the cosmos itself. The wilderness motif in Mark (Mark 6:31–32, 35; see Exodus 18:21; Numbers 27:17) alludes to the exilic hope of a second exodus at the end of days. "The way of the Lord" has a Deutero-Isaian meaning of a highway along which God himself moves as the invisible but powerful comforter of the afflicted, liberator of captives, and enlightener of the blind. Even in the earliest Gospel, exodus is an important paradigm.

In sum, the Christian Bible itself views the founding moment of Israel—the exodus, comprising liberation from false deities and formation into a people—as constitutive of Israel and capable of being renewed. Prophets interpreted each exodus, explaining the event and modeling the appropriate response to it. For Exodus I, Moses, a prophet prior to prophecy, explained in detail what was at stake and how to respond. For Exodus II, the prophets continued the Mosaic office, notably Hosea, Jeremiah, Ezekiel, and Second Isaiah. And for Exodus III, Jesus, the "eschatological prophet" (in the phrase of N. T. Wright), demonstrates by his teaching and deeds that he has brought the previous two exodus moments to their conclusion.

FURTHER READINGS

Allen, Ronald J., and Clark M. Williamson. *Preaching the Old Testament: A Lectionary Commentary*. Louisville: Westminster John Knox, 2007. On the Revised Common Lectionary.

Boisclair, Regina A. *The Word of the Lord at Mass: Understanding the Lectionary*. Chicago: Liturgy Training Publications, 2015.

Bonneau, Normand. *The Sunday Lectionary: Ritual Word, Paschal Shape*. Collegeville, MN: Liturgical Press, 1998.

Clifford, Richard J. "The Exodus in the Christian Bible: the Case for 'Figural' Reading." *Theological Studies* 63, no. 2 (2002): 345–61.

———. "Isaiah 40–55." In *The Jerome Biblical Commentary for the Twenty-First Century*. Edited by John J. Collins, Gina Hens-Piazza, Barbara Reid, OP, and Donald Senior, CP. London: T&T Clark, forthcoming.

Fishbane, Michael A. *Haftarot: the Traditional Hebrew Text with the New JPS Translation*. Philadelphia: The Jewish Publication Society, 2002. A masterful and detailed commentary on the Haftorah, the short reading from the Prophets that follows the reading from the Law (Torah) in synagogue worship.

Just, Felix, SJ. *The Catholic Lectionary Website*. https://catholic-resources.org/Lectionary (as of March 2021). Magnificent resource on the Catholic lectionary with links to a wide variety of online sources.

Leclerc, Thomas L. *Introduction to the Prophets: Their Stories, Sayings, and Scrolls*. New York: Paulist, 2007.

Martini, Carlo Maria, and Vera Castelli Theisen. *A Prophetic Voice in the City: Meditations on the Prophet Jeremiah*. Collegeville, MN: Liturgical Press, 1997. Remarkable blend of spiritual and critical reading of the prophet.

Pontifical Biblical Commission. *The Interpretation of the Bible in the Church*. Boston: Pauline Books and Media, 1996.

Seitz, Christopher R., ed. *Reading and Preaching the Book of Isaiah*. Philadelphia: Fortress Press, 1988. Collection of essays.

Tisdale, Leonora Tubbs, and Carolyn J. Sharp. "The Prophets and Homiletics." In *The Oxford Handbook of Prophecy*, 627–651. Edited by Carolyn J. Sharp. New York: Oxford University Press, 2016. Though primarily on preaching the prophets, it deals with liturgy also.

Wagner, J. Ross. "The Prophets in the New Testament." In *The Oxford Handbook of Prophecy*, 373–387. Edited by Carolyn J. Sharp. New York: Oxford University Press, 2016. Recent treatment of how the New Testament writers interpreted the prophets.

United States Conference of Catholic Bishops (USCCB): https://bible.usccb .org. Biblical readings for each day.

West, Fritz. *Scripture and Memory. The Ecumenical Hermeneutic of the Three-Year Lectionaries*. Collegeville, MN: Liturgical Press, 1997.

ABOUT THE COVER ART

Courtesy, National Gallery of Art, Washington. Andrew W. Mellon Collection.

These panels of the prophets Isaiah and Ezekiel on the cover of this book were originally part of a famous altarpiece painted for the cathedral in Siena, Italy, in 1311 by the early Renaissance painter Duccio di Buoninsegna (1255–1319). The prophets stood on either side of a nativity scene. The three panels appeared on the lower left of the altarpiece, in a row of scenes on the predella, or platform, on which a much larger panel of the altarpiece stood. In that main panel, often called the *Maestà*, or Majesty, the Virgin is enthroned, holding the Christ child, and surrounded by saints.

Isaiah's scroll bears an inscription (Isaiah 7:14) that translates "And a virgin will conceive and bear a son and his name will be Emmanuel." The inscription on Ezekiel's scroll (from Ezekiel 44:2) is "This gate shall be kept shut; it shall not be opened, and no man may pass through it."